Team Management
secrets
The experts tell all!

D1494762

About the author

Rus Slater is a management consultant and trainer in the UK who has worked in many areas of industry, commerce and public service. He is also the author of *Getting Things Done* and *People Management*, also in the **business secrets** series.

Author's note

This book is dedicated to Alexander and Frederick Slater.

Team Management
secrets

Collins

A division of HarperCollins*Publishers*

77-85 Fulham Palace Road, London W6 8JB

www.BusinessSecrets.net

First published in Great Britain in 2010 by HarperCollins*Publishers*
Published in Canada by HarperCollins*Canada*. www.harpercollins.ca
Published in Australia by HarperCollins*Australia*. www.harpercollins.com.au
Published in India by HarperCollins*PublishersIndia*. www.harpercollins.co.in

1

Copyright © HarperCollins*Publishers* 2010

SECRETS and BUSINESS SECRETS are trademarks of HarperCollins*Publishers*

Rus Slater asserts the moral right to be identified as the author of this work.

A catalogue record for this book is available from the British Library.

ISBN 978-0-00-734112-2

Printed and bound at Clays Ltd, St Ives plc

Mixed Sources
Product group from well-managed
forests and other controlled sources
www.fsc.org Cert no. SW-COC-001806
© 1996 Forest Stewardship Council

FSC is a non-profit international organisation established to promote the
responsible management of the world's forests. Products carrying the FSC
label are independently certified to assure consumers that they come
from forests that are managed to meet the social, economic and
ecological needs of present and future generations.

Find out more about HarperCollins and the environment at
www.harpercollins.co.uk/green

Contents

Managing teams is a balancing act

When you manage a team you are judged by your boss and by the team you manage. You are judged on the achievement of targets and your success as a people-manager, both of individuals and of the team as a whole. Managing teams is therefore a huge challenge. It is also a hugely rewarding career!

I first became a manager of a team in the 1970s and in the early days I made every mistake imaginable! In the 1980s I trained properly in team management and leadership and had a lot more success. Since then, I've managed formal and informal teams, teams of volunteers and staff, virtual teams and cross-functional teams.

In the 1990s I started designing and delivering training events in the management of teams for public and private sector organizations. This gave me a further insight beyond my own direct experience, in the pitfalls and possibilities of team management.

This book is a distillation of what I have learned over the years about managing teams. The book contains 50 **secrets** about the successful management of teams, which, if you follow them, will save you and your teams from a lot of misery. The secrets are organized into seven themed chapters.

■ Is this a team? You need to ensure that you have a team, not just a bunch of people! This is the foundation of getting it right.

■ Form your team. Teams don't just happen by chance; you have to work to create a team. That means you have to understand about teams, not just people.

■ Lead your team. If you are going to be a team manager then you have to lead them day-to-day. You can't sit back and rest on your laurels!

■ Communicate with your team. Most complaints about team managers relate to communication. It is a two-way process, and you have to get it right to be successful.

■ Protect and serve your team. You might be the one who gets paid more and has the bigger office, but your job is to protect and serve your team, not the other way round.

■ Manage team changes. Nothing stays the same for long. Teams change and the work changes. The team looks to you to manage them through the changes.

■ Disband your team. When the time comes, people don't like to leave without saying goodbye. If you manage the team disbandment well, the future opportunities are greater for all.

Whether you have been managing teams for a while or are a new leader, you will find that by using these secrets your people will follow you far more readily and willingly than if you don't.

The way you manage teams affects lots of people; it also affects your standing in the world.

Is this a team?

You may have the title of 'team manager' or 'team leader', but that doesn't mean you actually have a 'team'! A team has characteristics that set it apart from being just a group of people. If you don't recognize these characteristics, your team might fragment, or the work won't be done, or you might even find that a charismatic member of the team will actually become the real team manager whilst you flounder at the edge!

1.1

Know what you mean by 'team'

First of all, you need to be sure that you have a real team and not simply a group of people who have been put into the same room/organization/coloured shirt! Make sure you have a clear understanding of what a 'team' is from the outset.

There are several definitions for the word 'team', depending on different situations. For example, the Massachusetts Institute of Technology defines a team as: 'People working together in a committed way to achieve a common goal or mission. The work is interdependent and team members share responsibility and hold themselves accountable for attaining the results.'

Shorter definitions simply refer to a group of people and a common goal. Some definitions include interdependence of team members rather than the ability to function alone. Some add the requirement for team members to work cooperatively or harmoniously, defining the style of the interaction as well as the actuality. A team may be created for a specific task or it may have a longer lifespan. Some definitions include mutual accountability and responsibility for a team.

"I realised that I did not so much "lead a team" as preside over a bunch of egos"

Anonymous manager in the banking industry

From this you can see that although individual definitions of 'team' show some variation, there are some fairly universal concepts, which can be defined as:

- Teams have a common goal or purpose.
- Teams have more than one member.
- Teams have complementary skills and abilities.
- Teams work together.

So before you read any further in this book, ask yourself:

- "Do I have a group of people who all know that they actually belong to one team?" *(Have you checked?)*
- "Do they all have a common purpose that is clear, articulated and understood by all?" *(Are you sure?)*
- "Are they a group of people who have complementary skills and abilities?" *(Or have they actually been bunched together because they all have the same skills and knowledge.)*
- "Do they work together and depend on each other?" *(Or do they just work in the same place, each doing their own thing?)*

Don't assume you have a team until you have common agreement that this group of people is a team.

1.2

Define success for your team

Whether you have a sales team, a customer service team, a medical team, a combat team or a soccer team, there are certain characteristics that the team will need in order to be successful both in terms of how it operates and in relation to its achievement of targets.

1 There is clarity of purpose; members can and will commit themselves to the overall objectives.

2 The team has a clear, explicit and mutually agreed approach: conventions, norms, expectations and rules.

3 The individuals have clear performance goals against which they are measured. These may include a continuous series of milestones along the way to larger goals.

4 The atmosphere tends to be informal and there are no serious tensions. It is a working atmosphere in which people are involved and interested.

5 The team members listen to each other, and new ideas are openly discussed. Everyone has a say.

6 People are welcome to express their feelings about different issues as well as their ideas.

7 Disagreements are carefully examined and resolved rather than crushed. Dissenters are not seen as trying to dominate the group, but as having a genuine difference of opinion.

8 Each individual team member is respectful of the mechanics of the group: arriving on time, coming to meetings prepared, completing agreed upon tasks on time, etc.

9 Constructive feedback is welcomed, and it should be frequent, frank and relatively comfortable – oriented towards improving performance rather than allocating blame.

10 Whilst a single person may have the title of Team Leader, he or she may step quietly aside to allow others to work to their strengths. The issue is not who's in control at any particular moment, but how to get the job done.

Think about how your people will operate successfully as a team.

1.3

Know when you haven't got a team

There are numerous reasons why some groups calling themselves a team aren't really a team. This may not be a problem, but sometimes it is. Teambuilding with a group can be counter-productive, detracting from individual performance without any compensatory collective benefit.

A sales 'team' where the individuals work in *competition* with each other is not a real team. In this environment, the nature of competition and performance-related reward actively discourage team working in favour of an individual meritocracy. In a different example, an accounts office might contain a bought ledger 'team' of clerks. However, they all have the same role and so are not complementing each other's

case study In the early 20th century, when the explorer Ernest Shackleton was selecting his team for the Endeavour Expedition, he expressly selected beyond technical competence in the specific functions, actively seeking people who showed personality traits that he

skills within the 'team'. To recruit for either of the above examples is relatively straightforward: find people with exactly the same knowledge and skill and the job is virtually done!

A team, on the other hand, can be much more difficult to form:

■ Members of a team are selected for their complementary skills, not a single commonality. A business team may consist of an accountant, three sales people, a warehouseman, a delivery driver and a secretary, for example.

■ Each member of the team has an individual purpose and function relevant to the team's overall objective. This means that there will be interdependencies between team members.

■ The success of these interdependencies relies to a greater or lesser extent upon the relationships and interactions between the team members. There is usually not as much room for conflict when working as a team, or for independence. This creates challenges in selecting team members; do you select complementary personalities or people who have a lot in common?

Complementary skills and interdependencies make a real team; otherwise, 'team' is just a label.

felt would complement each other in the challenging environment that he knew was coming. Nowadays, a team manager has more objective tools at his or her disposal to help with this, such as psychometric assessments and 'team roles' questionnaires.

1.4

Plan to be a real team leader

There are lots of people in the world who use the title of Team Manager or Team Leader but are not genuinely doing anything to lead or manage. Sometimes this is a pure sinecure, while in other cases these people are deluding themselves.

Sinecure Team Leaders/Managers

People may be given the title of Team Manager as a sinecure (See Jargon buster) so that the organization can push them to the sidelines or a position where they can do no damage.

Sometimes this action follows the concept of the so-called 'Peter Principle', where a person has been promoted to a level beyond their competence. If no-one has the strength to remove them, they may be given a grand-sounding job title and marginalized. On the other hand, many organizations give sinecure job titles as a genuine way of recognizing and retaining technical talent. "We need to keep this person and give them more status, so we will call them a team leader but we don't actually expect team management from them."

Delusional Team Leaders/Managers

There are two types of delusional non-managers:

1 **People who have always viewed a management role as a 'privilege without responsibility'.** They get the bigger salary and the executive car parking space, and believe their job will be easy because people will automatically respect their rank and status. These people can usually be spotted by their absence! When they are around they have a tendency to 'throw their weight around'; they bluster and coerce their staff to do their bidding, which often has more to do with bolstering their own egos than with achieving any meaningful objectives.

2 **People who genuinely believe they are 'managing' but are really getting in the way of people doing their jobs.** These people can usually be spotted by their constant calls for progress reports, their insistence on holding meetings in which nothing is agreed, and their micro-management of staff in the mistaken belief that they are somehow "helping". They regularly introduce new initiatives, but rapidly lose interest in them.

If you have ever seen the TV sitcom called 'The Office' (either the original British version or the US spin-off) you will recognize the delusional type described here!

Your team will soon notice if you are a delusional team manager.

1.5

Check that you have some followers

If leadership is 'the relationship between those who choose to lead and those who choose to follow', then it is as important for a team to have followers as it is for the team to have a leader.

'Followership', however, is seldom an act of blind faith and unquestioning obedience (at least not in business), but a set of behaviours and characteristics that have been summed up by Keith Morgan (2005), who identified key elements that underpin effective followership.

■ Effective followers know what's expected of them; they make sure that their role/tasks have been clearly communicated to them and that they are clear about their responsibilities.
■ Effective followers seek to establish and maintain lines of two-way communication to reduce the risk of unclear messages.
■ Effective followers take initiative, keeping their leader informed. This is not just about personal action but may involve influencing other people.
■ Effective followers challenge flawed plans. This is one of the most valuable contributions that can be made by an effective follower. It is also one of the most difficult, since there is a risk of appearing negative, or distrustful of the leader's judgement.

"There go the people. I must follow them, for I am their leader"

Attributed to Ledru-Rollin (1807–74), French radical politician

■ Effective followers provide accurate feedback to their leader and their colleagues. This means providing both good and bad news in a timely, diplomatic and honest way.

■ Effective followers support the leader's efforts – all leaders need support and encouragement. This also means acting as advocates among their peer group and attempting to quash rumours.

It is a managerial responsibility to create an environment that encourages followership. This table summarizes the ideal conditions and behaviours of the followers and manager:

Behaviour of effective followers	Provisions made by effective manager	Behaviour of effective manager
They are clear about role and responsibilities.	Unambiguous goals and objectives.	Is open to requests for clarification or reasoning.
They maintain two-way communication.	Regular, frequent and relevant messages.	Asks questions and listens to answers.
They challenge flawed plans.	Opportunities and environments where challenges can take place.	Welcomes challenges, explains rationales, and is willing to rewrite plans without being defensive.
They provide accurate feedback.	Opportunities for frequent feedback.	Welcomes feedback, acts on feedback, and doesn't take it personally.
They support the leader's efforts.	A private place for team members to meet.	Rewards loyalty.

Effective 'followership' is a prerequisite of effective team management.

1.6

Manage a crossfunctional team

Many teams are cross-functional: they are made up of people from different departments or functions or even organizations. In this situation, each person has a part-time role on this team and another job elsewhere. It is crucial that you take this into account.

If your team members have another regular role elsewhere, then they also have a regular line manager, regular teammates, regular objectives and regular loyalties. This is referred to as a 'matrix organization'. The different lines of management and responsibilities make it much easier for people to become overloaded, distracted or confused, and conflicts of interest are much more likely.

In order to minimize the likelihood of problems with a crossfunctional team, you need to work hard on six areas of your management skills. You will notice that the initial letters of these skill areas spell **TOPCAT**.

■ **T = Team building.** You have to work really hard at this because your team members are already members of other teams. They already have a team identity and team loyalties elsewhere and these continue throughout the lifetime of your team. You need to balance getting them involved in your team without appearing to be trying to break them away from their other teams.

■ **O = Objective setting.** You not only have to set clear, unambiguous SMART objectives (see Jargon buster), but you have to do this in conjunction with the objectives and deadlines that your team members have in their other teams. This requires constant review and adjustment as well as extra liaison with team members and their other bosses.

■ **P = Performance feedback.** No one wants to be unappreciated, especially when a team member might be unpopular with their line manager for being 'absent-on-duty' with your team. Therefore, performance feedback is critical. If people are doing well, tell them (also tell their line manager). If they are not doing so well ask them what else they need from you in order to perform.

■ **C = Communication.** If you don't see your team members on a day-to-day basis, or they don't see each other each day, you have to keep everyone informed of activities, successes, problems, solutions, changes and everyday news. But you have to avoid overloading people who might be getting similar updates from their other teams!

■ **A = Arbitration.** You can't expect your team members to negotiate for your benefit with their other boss; you are going to have to do a lot of arbitration for your team members' time and resources. You will have to do this at the outset, when you set objectives, and frequently throughout the life of the team.

■ **T = Tackling conflict.** Life in a matrix organization is full of potential conflict. You are naturally going to feel that your team is the most important, while every other manager is naturally going to feel the same way about their team!

Be a TOPCAT to manage a cross-functional team successfully.

Form your team

If you are lucky you will be able to hand-pick people for your team. Otherwise, you will have to work with whoever is allocated. Either way, it is your responsibility to create 'esprit de corps'. This French term means a 'spirit of belonging in a group'. It applies when the team members know what to do and what not to do; they take pride in being part of the team; and they have the confidence to rely on their teammates.

2.1

Pick the right people

If you are given the opportunity to pick people for your team, then you need to take care in choosing people who will not only have the technical competence to do the job but who will also work harmoniously with their colleagues and you.

■ **Recruit for harmony.** You will actually need to consider how similar you want your team members to be to each other (or you!). Whilst there are benefits in getting people of the same mindset as each other, there are also tensions associated with having too many similarities between team members. For example, a team of 26 people who are all articulate, self-confident, ambitious, imaginative and highly motivated to be in the limelight can rapidly descend into a squabbling bunch of pushy people competing with one another to get promoted!

case study I was contracted to recruit a training specialist for a UK company. The initial request asked for candidates to be female graduates aged between 28 and 35 on the grounds that the team members were all female, all graduates aged under 33 and the team manager herself was 36. However, I put forward

■ **Think about strengths and weaknesses.** Within a perfect team there is a balancing act between individuals who get on together and individuals who bring specific strengths to the team. For example, on a football team you need to have a goalkeeper, some defenders, midfielders and strikers. You also need a balance of players who are good in the wet and some in the dry; some who play well when you are winning and some who shine when you are in trouble; some passionate players and some who are calm and methodical.

■ **Think about the environment.** In a car sales environment, for example, you might want people who are self motivated, use their initiative, take calculated risks and solve their own problems. If you are building a team to run a nuclear power station then you probably want a mix of methodical, exacting, analytical and risk-averse people.

■ **Take inspiration from other teams.** Many famous teams are made up of complementary characters. Think about the Magnificent Seven (gunfighters in the film), Wallace and Gromit (man and dog in animation series), Laurel and Hardy (comedy duo), the Dirty Dozen (assassins in the film), Hillary and Tenzing (real-life conquerors of Mount Everest), and even the 'A' Team (fugitive heroes in TV series).

Recruit great people to accomplish great things.

a shortlist that included a 42-year-old male ex-soldier who fulfilled all other criteria for the post. At interview he demonstrated a maturity and outlook different to the others in the team, and the company realized that he would provide a new perspective. He was recruited and quickly became a successful team member.

2.2

Get the team performing quickly

There are a number of preliminary stages before a team can start performing properly. The stages can be summarized as forming, storming, norming and performing. These stages sometimes happen naturally, but it is far better to manage them from the outset.

1 **Forming stage.** Team members identify each other by name, role and history. In order to get this stage successfully completed as quickly as possible, hold a proper 'forming' meeting – get everyone to introduce themselves and share this information.

2 **Storming stage.** The stage where, confident they are meant to be here, people start to 'jockey for position' – to establish their credibility in the team. Some will try to push themselves forward

case study A manager asked me to run a teambuilding course for his part-time IT project team. The team had spent 11 months and many thousands of pounds but had achieved nothing at all. Over two days of teambuilding, the team members properly introduced

because they want power or influence; others will deliberately keep a low profile because they are shy, diffident or lacking in confidence. You need to set up activities that allow people to find their level of comfort – for example any of the teambuilding exercises you can find on websites such as www.businessballs.com.

3 **Norming stage.** This is when you start to establish the rules of behaviour between team members, and their relationships with you and people outside. The Norming phase can take quite a long time if left to happen naturally because the rules will be established by a combination of 'trial and error' and 'custom and practice'. Take control by holding a team meeting to set up some formal ground rules. See Secret 2.5 for more details.

4 **Performing stage.** The team finally starts working effectively towards its goals. For example, a soccer team is performing when it is playing well – tackling, keeping possession, winning ground, supporting each other – even before it starts scoring goals.

Once you reach this stage you want to stay there! Follow the secrets in Chapters 3, 4, 5 & 6.

Don't let your team go through the first three stages without intervention; make them happen quickly and successfully.

themselves to each other for the first time; they did a couple of exercises that allowed them to 'storm'; and they produced their own team charter. They went on to achieve more in the following six weeks than they had in the previous 11 months.

2.3

Create a team identity

Effective teams nearly always have a team name, whether its Manchester United (football team), Greenpeace (environmental action group), the Rajasthan Royals (cricket team) or even the Beatles (pop band)! Nearly all teams have a logo and a unique style or uniform. A team identity gives individuals a powerful sense of belonging.

Even if the team you run is scattered across several departments of your organization, you can give them a sense of shared identity, such as with a team name, team logo, team motto, team vision and even a team 'strip' or uniform. Hold a team meeting and propose the idea: people will probably like it and be happy to choose or vote for things.

■ **Team name.** Keep it short and simple, for example The 'Hey!' Team rather than the Global Internal Corporate Communications Team. Go for something descriptive of the team's role or style, e.g. The Paper Tigers for an archive team. Try to find something different or even unique. Whereas lots of organizations have a Quality Team, why not call it The DRiFTers, standing for Do it Right First Time? Alliterative or punning names are usually successful, e.g. the Rajasthan Royals or Coach and Courses for your training team. Also make sure the name is easy to pronounce and spell in the language your team uses – a good example of a 'team' that adopted an easier name identity is the British Royal Family, who changed their surname from Saxe-Coburg-Gotha to Windsor in 1917.

■ **Team logo.** A logo can be used to add distinction to your workplace, your paperwork and yourselves. You need to keep the logo simple so that it remains recognizable when reduced in size on memos or polo shirts. Ideally have one designed in primary colours so it can be easily replicated if you want to have it embroidered, painted or printed, or just have a black and white logo, so it can easily be photocopied. Often the simplest shapes make the strongest icons – consider, for example, the Red Cross and Red Crescent.

■ **Team 'strip'.** You can create a team identity with clothing and accessories, such as hats, polo shirts, badges, buttons, umbrellas, document bags, and so on. Items such as these are all relatively cheap, unisex and often more popular and fun than a top-to-toe uniform.

■ **Team motto.** Take time to get the team together and challenge yourselves to come up with a good team motto. By 'good' you mean something that everyone will be proud to admit to! Keep it short and informative of the team ethos. Look at famous slogans for inspiration, such as Avis's *"We try Harder"*, General Electric's *"Imagination at Work"*; Barclays Bank's *"Fluid in Finance"*, or the British SAS's *"Who Dares Wins"*.

People like to be part of a team with a proper identity, so get them involved in creating that identity.

2.4

Create a team vision

A team is a group of people all trying to achieve one common objective, but the objective may change year on year. You need a bigger, aspirational 'vision' that encompasses but goes beyond the annual target.

■ A vision is the glue that binds the team together as each individual strives to achieve his or her personal goals.
■ A vision is what keeps you all focused on the 'big picture' when difficulties may otherwise seem insurmountable.
■ A vision is the fuel that motivates your people to achieve something that is truly challenging.

Depending on the ethos of the organization and the function of the team, your vision might range from the mercenary ("We are going to kill the competition"), through supportive ("We will be customers' supplier of choice") to the uplifting ("We will eradicate starvation")!
Here are some real examples of organizational visions:

■ **Google.** "To organize the world's information and make it universally accessible and useful."
■ **Microsoft (in the 1980s).** "A personal computer in every home running Microsoft software."
■ **Volunteer Reading Help.** "Confident children; literate for life."

Note that visions are future aspirations, not current descriptions. To create a vision ask yourself:

■ What do we really, really want to achieve?
■ What would make us feel really, really successful?
■ What do we want to remember about this team when we are old?
■ What could we do that would make us feel proud?
■ What would people remember us for?
■ What would make people want to erect a statue in our honour?

As you can see, 'people' in the last two questions could mean the citizens of your country, your children and grandchildren, your shareholders or customers. It will depend on the type of job you and your team do; commercial, public sector and medical teams will doubtless have different approaches, leading to different team visions.

You can undertake this exercise in isolation or you can get your team involved. Personally I'd recommend the latter; this way the team members contribute to a vision that they can genuinely believe in and support; otherwise it is your vision and not necessarily theirs.

Once everyone shares the vision then the values of the team, acceptable behaviours, appropriate goals and an atmosphere of mutual support follow.

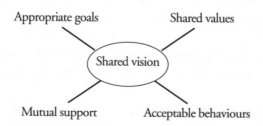

A shared vision means you are all facing the same way on the road to your goal.

2.5

Agree the ground rules

Ground rules should be set early to make it clear what behaviour is acceptable among members of the team, including you as the team leader. Depending on the circumstances, ground rules can also relate to other internal departments, customers, competitors, shareholders and so on.

It is better for your team to create the ground rules themselves rather than you imposing the rules upon them. This may seem counter-intuitive – you are, after all, supposed to be the leader – but you can lead the team to produce their own rules. Here's how to do it.

1 Get the team together, ideally away from the workplace but certainly somewhere where you can work without disturbance for a few hours.
2 Give everyone a pen and paper.
3 Ask each person to complete the following sentence: "I hope that X happens within this team." Ask them to do this alone, because you want individual answers not the consensus at this stage. People can write as many sentences as they want.

Typically the sort of answers you get will be: "That people will listen to me", "That people will tell the truth", "That everyone will work hard", "That credit will be given for success", and similar.

4 Write these answers onto a big flipchart sheet.
5 Now lead a discussion that relates to: "What must I do to make this hope a reality?" ("I" refers to each team member individually.) Make sure that you get the opinions of everyone in the team, not just the loudest or most senior. Make sure everyone is prepared to accept, abide by and support the wording of the 'Promise'.
6 As you complete each line, write in the 'Promises', as in the example below:

Hope	Promise
"That people will listen to me."	"I will say what I mean, at an appropriate time."
"That people will tell the truth."	"I will presume that people are telling the truth unless I have cause to believe otherwise."
"That everyone will work hard."	"I will work hard at my job and assist others where I can."
"That people will turn up on time."	"I will not waste other people's time by being late."

Once you have written up a 'promise' to go with each 'hope', you will have created a set of ground rules that everyone accepts.

Guide your team to set its own ground rules.

2.6

Understand team roles

Meredith Belbin's work at Henley Management College in England identified nine clusters of team behaviour, termed 'team roles'. Each role has its particular strengths and allowable weaknesses, and makes an important contribution to the team.

The nine roles that contribute to a successful team are:

■ **Specialist.** *Positive contribution:* Provides technical knowledge and skills, dedicated to his/her profession. *Probable weakness:* Narrow area of contribution; often ignores non-technical issues.

■ **Plant.** *Positive contribution:* Ideas person; creative and a problem solver. *Probable weakness:* Bored by detail and incidentals.

■ **Shaper.** *Positive contribution:* Thrives on pressure. Dynamic; driven and determined to overcome obstacles. *Probable weakness:* Expects same level of drive from everyone; prone to upset people who don't have it.

■ **Co-ordinator.** *Positive contribution:* A good chairperson who clarifies goals, keeps people focused and promotes decision-making. Good at delegating. *Probable weakness:* Can be perceived as manipulative and controlling. Seen as lazy; gets others to do the work.

■ **Teamworker.** *Positive contribution:* Listens to others, builds consensus, acts as peacemaker and diplomat. *Probable weakness:* Indecisive when rapid action is needed.

■ **Monitor/evaluator.** *Positive contribution:* Sober, objective, analytical. *Probable weakness:* Seldom inspiring to others; may be perceived as negative.

■ **Implementer.** *Positive contribution:* Likes to get on with things; good at turning ideas into actions, and plans/strategies into realities. *Probable weakness:* Impatient; conservative in times of change.

■ **Resource investigator.** *Positive contribution:* Enthusiastic ambassador and communicator within and outside the team. Keen on opportunities. *Probable weakness:* Can be over-optimistic, often fails to see things through once everyone else is on board.

■ **Completer finisher.** *Positive contribution:* Painstaking and conscientious; always checking own and others' work; finishes on time. *Probable weakness:* Often worries; seldom delegates because rarely trusts others.

Most people naturally cover two or more team roles, so teams of three or four members can successfully have all roles represented.

Having a comprehensive covering of all the roles will provide a complete team. If any roles are missing, then the team will have a deficiency. A team with too much of one preference will probably develop an unhealthy culture. For example, a team with lots of 'resource investigators' is likely to create lots of ideas but fail to see them through to successful completion. A team without any 'plants' is likely to lack innovation; it will probably stagnate into a repetitive and plodding culture.

As the team manager you also have to manage the healthy frictions between the different types of people, which is what the next secret is all about!

Understanding team roles will help you and your team to value differences.

2.7

Use roles for teamwork and task success

Secret 2.6 introduced you to the theory behind team roles but what use is that to you? Firstly you need to know what team role preference each of your people has, then use this knowledge to help form, develop and manage your team.

You can find out people's preferences by getting them to take a team role questionnaire online, such as the one available from www.belbin.com. Alternatively, you can go on a more subjective approach based on your own judgement or people's own opinions.

Once you have an idea of peoples' natural inclinations, you can then use this knowledge to seek appropriate people to form your team or to join if your team is already in place. You can also use it at this stage to identify possible problems in the future.

---

case study A builder had problems relating to scaffolding collapsing mid-build. He discovered that the joints holding the towers together had not been tightened after levelling. For his next building project

---

■ **Devoping your people's team roles.** People's team roles are about personal preference rather than knowledge or ability, but you can still help to develop team members to lean more towards other team roles. For instance, training someone in presentation or communication skills can improve their confidence to a level where they enjoy the 'resource investigator' role. Similarly, giving someone the opportunity and support to manage team meetings may allow them to develop confidence and therefore a preference for 'co-ordinating' behaviours.

■ **Managing your people's team roles.** It is inevitable that there will be tensions within an effective team. The 'specialists' will resent the apparent 'limelight stealing' of the 'resource investigators'; the 'shapers' will be frustrated at the apparent 'plodding approach' of the 'completer finishers' and the 'negative attitude' of the 'monitor evaluators'... and you (hopefully a strong 'co-ordinator' type!) will be trying to manage the team by getting everyone to focus on the goals, make decisions and reach consensus!

By recognizing the different types, you can pre-empt some of the tensions by anticipating them and therefore using your own skills and preferences (as well as those of your teamworkers) to manage the level of tension to a healthy level.

By remaining aware of the differences in your team you can keep everyone working together.

he ensured that he had at least one completer/finisher on the scaffolding team who would never let anyone up the tower until he had personally checked and tightened each and every nut on the site!

2.8

Measure the teamwork

With the welter of pressures of work, customer demands, changing environment and targets to hit, it is easy to lose sight of your role as the team manager. You need to get to GRIPS with teamwork.

GRIPS stands for Goals, Roles, Interactions, Processes and Style. GRIPS is designed to assess and measure the team members' individual perceptions of the teamworking aspects of their life. The actual outcome of that teamworking is measured by achievement of goals.

■ **Getting started with GRIPS.** Your people need to understand that all feedback is welcome, and all feedback will be listened to. The objective of seeking the feedback is to help the team. We are not here to look at the achievement of goals, but at the teamwork.

People should complete the questionnaire on the next page with their 'first instinct' answers.

When you are analysing the scores it is important to capture and calculate:

■ The average score for each question.
■ The range of scores on each question.

TEAMWORK REVIEW METRIC

Review and score YOUR opinion of how well we are *performing as a team* (we are scoring our *teamworking*, not whether we are hitting our targets)

1=No way... 6=Definitely

GOALS	1	2	3	4	5	6
a) Do we have a COMMON understanding of our team goal?						
b) Do we have common COMMITMENT to our team goal?						
c) Do I have clear personal goals?						
ROLES						
d) Do we have a CLEAR allocation of roles?						
INTERACTIONS						
e) Do we communicate OPENLY to one another?						
f) Do we really LISTEN to what is said?						
g) Are we CONSTRUCTIVE about what we hear?						
h) Are appropriate people involved in making decisions?						
PROCESSES						
j) Do we plan our tasks?						
k) Do we use the most appropriate "tools" to plan and fulfil our tasks?						
m) Do we use the most appropriate resources (including people)?						
STYLE						
n) Is our leadership/management style conducive to good teamwork?						
p) Is my followership style conducive to good teamwork?						
q) Are my colleagues' followership styles conducive to good teamwork?						

The average will give an indication of the general perception of your team's performance in that area and the range will indicate the commonality of perception.

By looking at the average scores you can see the areas where there is room for improvement over the whole team. A small range tells you that the perception is shared, while a wide range tells you that someone in the team feels that they have been ignored, neglected or treated unfairly, which needs investigating.

Use a GRIPS questionnaire to measure teamwork.

2.9

Manage teams within teams

Your team probably sits within a larger corporate team, and within your team you may have smaller sub-teams. This situation can be managed in a healthy way or it can become destructive. It is your job to manage it.

■ **The 'silo' mentality.** An organization will have an overall objective and will see itself as one big team trying to achieve that goal. However, teams at departmental and function level often develop an unhealthy attitude of elitism that is detrimental to the organization as a whole. For example, sales teams that are rewarded well for winning business often develop a superior self-image over the operations teams who deliver that business to the customer. Each individual team is effective, but

case study A man was overheard in the lift complaining to his colleague that the accounts people were making his life a misery as usual. The person who overheard him was a senior accounts manager! That manager decided to invite other managers to send people to what he called a 'Dilo Day' (Day In the Life

together they are constantly engaged in a series of little battles. This is sometimes referred to as a 'silo mentality' – each function within the business operates in its own 'silo' without connecting with the others.

■ **Cross-functional solution.** One way in which companies try to overcome this danger is to organize their team across functions (see Secret 1.6). Where this happens it is usually very effective. Sadly this is usually used solely as an ad hoc approach, such as for project teams and product launch teams, rather than a permanent organizational design.

■ **Inter-team competition.** Another idea is to arrange friendly competitions between your team and others. These can be work-related competitions with business-oriented targets such as revenue generation, customer satisfaction scores, output targets or speed of delivery. Or they can be social competitions such as softball or five-a-side. Some organizations hold competitions where each team picks a local charity and competes with the other teams to see who can raise the most money for their charity. The point about these inter-team competitions is that there is no 'cash prize' - they are done for fun.

■ **Co-operative approach.** Alternatively, nothing breaks down a silo mentality as well as secondments and job shadowing.

Find ways to avoid a 'silo mentality' with teams within teams.

Of...). Each visitor shadowed an accounts team member for a typical day. The programme created several changes in the accounts team process, suggested by their visitors, and several changes in processes and policies from other teams to allow them to work better with the accounts team.

Lead your team

This chapter aims to help you balance your workload so that you can actively manage your team without becoming stressed. It includes the secrets of creating tasks and giving instructions, generating team spirit and finding time to manage people. You will also discover how to avoid being a 'monkey manager'.

3.1

Create tasks

Each individual team member has personal tasks and objectives to fulfil in order to support the team. As the manager or leader of the team, it is your primary role to define these tasks and objectives.

This will include writing job descriptions that set out generic demarcations of responsibility, extracting individual targets from the team objectives, and agreeing developmental objectives for people to help them improve their skills and abilities.

■ **Defining tasks.** When writing job descriptions always refer the tasks of the individual to the team vision and objectives. If you don't do this the job can lose its apparent point. If a team member asks, for example: "Why do I have to keep the workshop clean and tidy?" Sample answers

case study A landowner had a problem: in the planting season he had work for 40 people, tilling, sowing and planting out. In the growing season he needed people for weeding and spraying. In the harvesting season he needed them for picking and packing. But in the winter there was nothing on the crops that needed doing. Yet he didn't want to lay off

without reference to the team vision or objectives might be: "Because that's what you're paid for!" "Because the quality manual demands it." Whereas the *real* reason is that having a clean and tidy workshop allows you to provide a better service to customers because it is safe and everything can be found quickly.

■ **Defining targets.** When extracting individual targets from team objectives make sure that you allocate targets fairly rather than necessarily equally. If you have people who are more experienced or who achieve results faster then it is fair to expect greater things from them than from those who are new to the task, work fewer hours or have other duties that reduce their ability to contribute.

■ **Agreeing developmental objectives.** Whenever you have the opportunity, arrange some job shadowing or secondments (Secret 2.9), set learning and development tasks, engage in teambuilding activities, work out process improvements (Secret 5.6) or even just find some 'make-work' tasks to keep your team busy. Thus, even during relatively quiet periods, people can improve their technical and communication skills and take on new responsibilities. It all goes towards keeping motivation high.

Busy teams are productive teams if you create meaningful tasks.

the workers in winter, partly from a sense of loyalty to them and partly because he didn't want to keep recruiting and training new people every spring. So in winter he had his staff pick pebbles from the local pond shore and lay miles of mosaic pathways around the estate. The landowner was popular with the locals, and his estate was both productive and attractive.

3.2

Build inter-dependencies

Teams consist of people working together, which means they need to work *inter-dependently*, rather than independently. Again it is your job as the team manager to ensure that there is inter-dependence between the team members in order to stop your team fragmenting.

When writing job descriptions make sure that you write each one with the others in mind so that the job descriptions of the team, linked together, cover the whole flow of the team's actions towards its objective. For instance:

■ The sales person's job description sets out their responsibility to agree a delivery time for the customer that the delivery person can achieve.
■ The delivery person's job description sets out their responsibility to get the proof of receipt that the sales ledger clerk needs to write the invoice.
■ The sales ledger clerk's job description sets out their responsibility to include the detail on the invoice that allows the customer to authorize the payment.

"Talent wins games, but teamwork and intelligence win championships"

Michael Jordan, American basketball player

When designing individual ad hoc tasks link them wherever possible to other tasks rather than making them stand alone. For instance:

■ "Jackie, I want you to research the market and collect data on competitor marketing for product X. That data is to be supplied to Chris by the 13th of October."

■ "Chris, I want you to take the information Jackie is collecting now, look at our marketing on product X, and assess it all to produce a comparison of the current marketing activity in the sector. This needs to be emailed to Les by the 21st of October."

■ "Les, I want you to take the comparison that Chris is providing and write some recommendations for our marketing activity on product X in order to help us to take advantage of the upcoming holiday season. I need this by the 7th of November."

By linking each task to other people the inter-dependencies are built. Alternatively, you can build inter-dependencies by creating a sub-team for specific tasks. For example:

■ "Chris Les, and Jackie, I want you all to produce some recommendations to help us take advantage of the holiday season with product X. I suggest that Jackie does the competitor research, Chris compares that data against our own activity and Les then writes some recommendations. I need the finished report by November the 7th."

The more people work together and rely on each other, the more your team functions successfully as a team.

3.3

Avoid MIYST

MIYST stands for Managing In Your Spare Time; in other words working a full day doing technical stuff and leaving any management activities before or after those hours. MIYST is a problem for a lot of team managers, particularly in situations where a technical specialist has been promoted to team manager.

In these instances the technical specialist may not really want to manage the team but to continue doing what he or she knows well – being a specialist. Moreover, some organizations discourage managers from real management activity by instigating 'charge time' to clients or to projects. This results in all staff having utilization targets.

case study In the early years of the new millennium, a large retail and distribution business in the UK recognized the need to improve the skills of their managers, and so provided an intensive training programme in team management and leadership. About halfway through the training programme, it was clear that there was a lot of cynicism among managers that they hadn't got the time to use all this management theory

For example, if a manager is expected to be 95% utilized, and works a 38-hour week, then he or she is only allowed to spend 114 minutes per week managing and the other 2166 minutes doing technical, client-paid work. That means less than 23 minutes per day spent managing or leading your team. If you have a team of six, this equates to less than 4 minutes per person per day!

In order to avoid MIYST you need to:

■ Manage your boss's expectations of you personally as well as of your team. To do this successfully you need to know what is going on in your team, think on your feet, be analytical and assertive (Secret 5.8).

■ Avoid being a 'monkey manager' (Secret 3.8). To do this successfully you have to practise 'tough love', break learned dependency, know your hot buttons and show faith in your people.

■ Delegate to support the team. In order to do this successfully you have to decide what can be delegated, to know how to delegate, and to be seen to be managing in the time you have saved yourself by delegating (Secret 3.9).

■ Use all available channels of communication to get your message across more quickly but just as effectively (Secret 4.2).

Don't underestimate the time needed to manage properly.

because of their utilization targets. There was much worry at senior executive level that giving managers 'time off' to manage would have a proportionate detrimental effect on productivity. Eventually it was agreed to reduce utilization for managers to 80 percent. Therefore, a full-time manager was allowed to manage for seven hours and forty minutes each week. Productivity rose by 18%!

3.4

Manage the miseries

There are some people who go around permanently complaining. On top of this, everyone has good days and bad days, and on the bad days we are miserable. As a manager it is your job to keep people as positive as possible, and that means managing the miseries.

When people look miserable, sound miserable or act in a miserable way it saps the energy of all around them. Whereas, when people exude energy and enthusiasm it tends to lift the spirits of all around and therefore not only makes life sweeter but encourages everyone to achieve greater things. Here are four ways to manage the miseries.

1 **Identify miserable behaviour.** Miserable behaviour will present itself in many ways. Glum, sad faces; slow dragging movements; slumped shoulders; complaining about everything (especially to people who can't change things); muttering under the breath; suspicion and an unwillingness to act.

2 **Isolate the miseries.** If you have a temporary misery (someone who is just having a bad day/week/month), get them on their own, away from the rest of the team so that you can talk to them privately. If you have a permanent misery (someone who normally exhibits glumness), keep them close to you, so that you

> "When you're chewing on life's gristle, don't grumble, give a whistle, and this'll help things turn out for the best" **From 'Always Look on the Bright Side of Life' by Eric Idle, British comedian**

can keep a closer eye on them than if they were elsewhere, infecting other team members with their negativity.

3 **Distract their negative thoughts.** Explain the positive rationale for tasks that otherwise seem pointless (never fall back to saying "because that is the rule" or "because I say so"). Ask their opinion or give them the choice of how to do tasks. If you have no tasks to give them, ask them what tasks they think would be beneficial. Get them to recast their negative thoughts by getting them to look on the 'bright side' of the issue; almost every issue can be seen as a problem or an opportunity, it is just that sometimes the opportunity is harder to see than the problem. For example, customers are complaining. Problem: we have to deal with unhappy customers. Opportunity: at least they are telling us what is wrong so we can put it right and keep their business.

4 **Remove the miseries.** Ultimately if you have a permanently miserable person who simply refuses to 'lighten up' and is dragging the morale and productivity of the team down, then remove them from your team.

There is only one thing more infectious than enthusiasm, and that is misery.

3.5

Keep smiling

You may be the team manager but you aren't a super-hero. You also have good days and bad days and you also have issues outside work that will affect your morale and possibly spill over into your work. You have to lead by example though, and you must therefore always present a positive front to your team.

If you find yourself sinking into a negative mental state, you need to revive yourself to restock your energy and spirit, and shift your mindset towards the positive. Indulge yourself in whatever is available to you to put the smile back on your face.

■ **Do something you really enjoy.** Personally I love walking and looking at the changing view. Ten minutes gets me over any short-term annoyance.

■ **Do something different.** A change is as good as a rest. Pick something else from your 'to do' list and go and do it for half an hour.

■ **Give yourself a treat.** Whatever is your personal favourite: chocolate, a cup of coffee, a head massage.

■ **'Get it off your chest.'** Find somewhere where you won't frighten anyone and have a half-minute yell! This will get rid of any pent-up aggression, and clear your mind and body.

"Perpetual optimism is a force multiplier"

Colin Powell, American statesman and general

■ **Get moving.** Exercise releases hormones that make you feel alive, refreshed, and energized. If you can't go for a proper work out, keep some stress toys handy for this type of occasion or even just a tennis ball to roll and bounce in your hands.

■ **Step out into the daylight.** That is why people refer to happy folk as having a 'sunny disposition'.

■ **If it's raining then go out in the rain.** It'll be so nice to get back into the dry again that you'll return to work feeling happier.

■ **Listen to music.** Put on something that you find personally energizing or invest in an uplifting compilation of music.

■ **Do a quick 'bad news, good news' activity.** For example, "The bad news is that I just got given a great big month-long report to prepare. The good news is I can guarantee I've got a job for at least a month and if I do a good job it may be an opportunity to show the boss how good I am."

■ **See your problem in the context of the wider world.** You are miserable because there is something wrong in your life, but stop and think of people who are worse off than you. It could be people you know or people in the news. You'll quickly find someone who is in a worse position than you. Take a moment to 'count your blessings'.

Having a positive mental attitude is a tremendously powerful force.

3.6

Give praise in public

Have you ever heard anyone say, "Everything must be fine, we haven't seen the boss in days"? Most people feel that their boss only really notices anyone in the team when there's something to complain about. This isn't motivating. When you manage a team you not only have to 'catch people doing things right', you also have to be seen to be doing it.

As the manager of a team, it is important that you are seen to fairly recognize good effort and good results. You have to 'catch people doing things right' in order to motivate individuals. To motivate the team and to develop and maintain team spirit you have to be seen to give positive feedback, equitably across the whole team. This does not mean that you have to offer praise to everyone, regardless of their effort or performance – that would be equal rather than fair.

To 'catch people doing things right' you simply need to remember to say "thanks" and "well done" every time someone completes a task, is seen to be working hard, helps someone out or fulfils an instruction. It is very easy in the busy day-to-day world to forget these simple courtesies, or to rationalize not using them on the grounds that people are just doing what they are paid to do.

one minute wonder Take a time each day to seek out some aspect of praiseworthy behaviour from your team. It can be anything from "thanks for all getting here on time" to "thanks for the care you are putting into this" or "well done for bringing the project in on time and to budget". Seek it out and praise it. Soon you will find that other people are actively seeking to copy the behaviour that they have seen you appreciate in others.

To generate the team ethos you need to be seen doing these things:

■ Say "thanks" and "well done" within earshot of other people.
■ Mention it in passing, casually, at appropriate times. For instance, "Here is the report you need to base your recommendations on. Dave has done a great job of collating all the data."
■ Send an email to say thanks and well done and cc or bcc it to other team members.
■ When holding team briefings (see Secret 4.1) add a word of praise to each appropriate aspect of the progress report.
■ If you use 'data display' (Secret 4.2) use it to provide written, public thanks.
■ Send thank you cards. People tend to pin them up over their workstation or on the team board.

Visible praise is shared recognition which, being shared, builds team spirit and cements behaviours that can be repeated and copied.

3.7

Reward your people

Rewarding your team can be trickier than you might imagine. If you reward people differently and get it 'wrong' then your team falls apart in jealousies and snobbery. If you reward everyone the same you may see a collapse in motivation as people see their contribution undervalued in relation to that of others.

That is why you may think yourself lucky that you have no control over the reward structure if you work for a large company that has set bandings or grading of staff and set pay scales within the bands/grades. For the purposes of this secret we are going to presume that you don't have the authority to set pay rates and offer wage increases. (If you do have control over people's wages then that warrants a whole book of its own, and there are some recommendations in the Further Reading section at the end of this book.)

case study A manager was tearing his hair out over the fact that team meetings always dragged on for ages with lots of interesting but irrelevant discussion. He set a new timed agenda and introduced it to the

■ Recognize team members' effort or success with printed certificates expressing your appreciation.

■ For special team occasions, such as the completion of a project or hitting targets, treat the team to an informal meal out.

■ For someone's birthday, bring in a cake and celebrate.

■ Have a visible bulletin board where you can post 'recognition' notes. Put up any letters of appreciation or any compliments that any member of the team gets from customers, internal or external.

■ Hand-write a personal note of thanks for a job well done. This includes a person who has improved previous poor performance.

■ Give a 'free' day off in recognition of outstanding achievement (be sure to check your HR rules on this one first).

■ Print 'escape vouchers' for 'one free hour off', '30-minute late start', and '30 minute early home' to reward exceptional behaviour. (You could model it on the 'Get Out of Jail Free Card' in Monopoly!)

■ Set a meaningful team target with a defined reward.

■ Go for 'planned spontaneous recognition'. It is planned because you know what you are looking for in terms of team behaviour; it is spontaneous because you haven't told the team. "Chris, you answered that phone before it had rung three times, that was great, thanks, have a Mars Bar on me!"

■ Give the 'supporting' reward. "Hi Chris, I noticed you haven't left your desk for three hours. You're working so hard, I brought you a coffee and a doughnut!"

Small rewards can mean a lot to staff.

team with a promise that if everyone stuck to it there would be a big box of chocolates as a reward. He started the meeting with the chocolates on the table and a clock on top of them. They finished on time!

3.8

Avoid being a 'monkey manager'

When a manager takes unresolved work from a team member, a figurative monkey leaps from the team member's back to that of the manager. If you have too many monkeys, you can't work effectively.

Examples of team members attempting to 'pass a monkey':
■ "Hi Jo, Steve won't give me the data I need for my report – can you speak to him for me?"
■ "I need a 16mm widget but they haven't got any in the store…"
■ "My PC isn't talking to the printer. Can you run these off on your machine, please?"

The team member who brings the monkey has the ability to solve the problem but lacks the empowerment, self-belief or will to do so. Instead of accepting the monkey yourself, you need to 'feed the monkey' together. Here are some points to bear in mind.

1 **Don't let the monkey jump.** At no time whilst you are helping a team member should you let their problem actually become your problem. They should be allowed to ask for your help, but you must not let the monkey jump.

2 **Monkeys should be fed or shot.** A problem not solved/work not done has consequences. If the package of work or problem cannot be solved immediately then a feeding time and schedule needs to be established.

3 **The monkey population should be kept below the maximum number that the manager has time to feed.** The originators of the monkey analogy suggest that it should take 15 minutes to feed a single monkey, and that managers should keep the list of problems that are in various stages of solution at a manageable number.

4 **Monkeys should be fed by appointment only.** Allowing team members to bring monkeys to you at their convenience increases the chances that the monkey will jump. By refusing to feed monkeys on-demand you empower team members to make interim decisions about the problem, and still report back.

5 **Monkey feeding times may be rescheduled but never cancelled unless the monkey dies.** The manager or team member may postpone a feeding time for any reason, but it must be rescheduled to avoid losing track of the monkey.

6 **All monkey-related activity must take place verbally – never in writing.** Holding feeding sessions via e-mail, letter or memo transfers the monkey to the manager by default. Feedings that take place verbally prevent the monkey from jumping unless the team manager makes a definite action to take it.

Help people to feed their own monkeys.

3.9

Delegate to support your team

There are lots of reasons to delegate tasks and responsibilities. Good delegation utilizes people's strengths, weeds out weaknesses, spreads the workload equitably, maximizes output, develops a multi-skilled team, shows trust in people, encourages responsibility and prepares people for promotion. Delegation is an essential part of managing your team.

In Secret 2.6 you learned about 'team roles' and hopefully you have a strong preference for being a co-ordinator. Remember, a good chairperson clarifies goals, keeps people focused, promotes decision-making and is good at delegating. However, this person can also sometimes be perceived as manipulative, controlling and lazy, sneakily getting others to do the work. Fear of this negative viewpoint makes a lot of managers unwilling to delegate work. But, if you are the team manager, you fill up the time you gain from delegation with management, and management is, of course, work!

If you delegate tasks effectively, you should then use the time you personally 'save' to do these other things: arranging monkey-feeding sessions, catching people doing things right, communicating with your team, carrying out public relations activities on behalf of the team, supporting individual team members, managing the miseries, measuring the teamwork and managing your boss. You will be able to support your team far more effectively in this way than if you are permanently tied up with problem-solving and technical stuff.

In order to delegate effectively, you need to ensure that the team member you delegate to has the four **STAR** elements of Skill, Time, Authority and Responsibility.

1   **S = Skill.** Though you may be delegating a task in order to help someone develop the skill, you obviously have to ensure that they have an adequate level of ability for the standard you agree and the time you allow. For example, with someone who has never done this specific task before, you may allow a lower standard (draft rather than final document for example) or more time than you might if you were delegating the task to someone with a proven track record.

2   **T = Time.** Not only the time for this specific task, as mentioned above, but in relation to their other workload.

3   **A = Authority.** If the person is reliant on others and does not usually have the authority then they need to be given 'acting rank' or a letter of authority or a licence. Otherwise they will not get the support they need.

4   **R = Responsibility.** The person to whom you delegate a task has to know that they will be held responsible for its completion. Without responsibility, motivation may be very hard to find. "Why bother?" will be the likely attitude.

If you aren't delegating, you're probably barely managing the team.

Communicate with your team

Employee surveys often show that poor communication is a problem in the workplace. Setting up a culture in which you listen to your team is just as important as talking to them. In this chapter you will find useful ways to ensure that team communication is planned, controlled and highly effective. There are also tips that will help you to communicate with external people on behalf of your team, protecting them from the vagaries of insignificance.

4.1

Run good team briefs

'Team briefs' is a concept that originated in the UK in the 1960s, before the advent of the mobile phone and Internet. It helps in the management of communications up and down the line in large organizations. The concept also works at team level.

Team briefing happens when a team manager arranges to meet regularly with the team to talk about what is happening in the workplace. The principles of good team briefs are that they:

■ **Are face-to-face.** In the modern world this may also mean via teleconference or videoconference.
■ **Take place at a whole team level.** No opt-outs allowed.
■ **Are led by the team leader.** Though team members can be delegated to chair individual meetings for developmental purposes.
■ **Follow a common agenda.** The team gets used to it and knows what to expect.
■ **Happen on a regular and frequent basis.** Weekly or monthly team briefings can be good, whereas daily would likely be too much, and quarterly probably not enough.

■ **Include both organizational and team items, formal and informal.** You can discuss targets and budgets, other business of the organization, staff social issues and team member news.

■ **Encourage feedback from the team.** This is a good opportunity for the team manager to get feedback about teamwork and his or her management style. You can focus on GRIPS (Secret 2.8) in a team brief. It is also a good place to seek opinions, suggestions and requests for more information to pass back up the line to senior management.

Where team briefs can go wrong	*What you can do about the problem*
Seen as a time-wasting activity.	Keep the meetings short.
Used simply to cascade information down.	Ask open questions regarding what people want to feed back; set exercises to share opinions.
Insufficient preparation.	Lead by example; send out agendas in advance; give clear instructions about preparation.
The information is not relevant to the audience.	Cull it in your preparation; cut short irrelevant discussions; 'park' for discussion elsewhere any subjects that are relevant but too long or of minority interest.
Failure to answer or follow up feedback.	Follow up what's in your control; chase those that aren't in your direct power.

Provide information and the opportunity for people to express views and ask questions. But remember, 'brief' means brief!

4.2

Use all channels to give your message

The most obvious way to communicate is to talk with people but there are many other channels of communication. Make sure that the methods you employ all work well.

You will know your people, your preferred style of communicating and the style of your organization, so use your judgement to assess what combination of media is appropriate for each message you want to get across. Try to avoid always using every medium for every message: this is a method adopted by some lazy managers, but it leads to information overload and is also prone to the same message being presented slightly differently in different media, resulting in mixed interpretations.

You also need to be aware of who you *don't* want to send the message to. For example, bulletin boards in places that can be seen by customers may be a bad place to put anything that relates to sales targets.

Surprisingly, while received wisdom is that people prefer the one-to-one informal discussion or the team meeting, it is recognized that the other media mentioned opposite are all seen as valid ways to communicate in the workplace.

Medium	Potential benefit	Potential weakness
Informal one-to-one discussion.	Immediate, live response; personal and confidential.	Not auditable; you have to be prepared for and willing to accept the immediate response.
Team meeting/team brief.	Regular, common message to all; engenders team ethos; auditable; live response.	Seen as a waste of time; info not relevant to all; used only to cascade info; requires preparation.
Bulletin board/data display.	Permanently visible; reinforces message; visible to others.	Open to people outside the team (perhaps); can become 'wallpaper' (people don't notice it).
Guest speaker.	Adds weight to message.	Unprepared guest speakers can do damage.
Email.	Immediate send; auditable; can be one-to-one or for whole team.	Open to misinterpretation.
Handwritten note/memo/card.	Personal; informal; confidential if in an envelope.	Probably not auditable (you don't tend to keep a copy of a note).
Phone call.	Immediate, live response; personal; confidential.	Not auditable; you have to be prepared for and willing to accept the immediate response.
Conference call.	Common message; engenders team ethos; live response; can be auditable.	Easy to attribute comment to wrong people; requires some skill to manage; reliant on technology.
Video conference.	Common message; engenders team ethos; live response; can be auditable.	Requires lots of technology.
Text message.	Immediate; auditable; personal.	'Predictive text' can send wrong words; seen as impersonal for important matters.

Choose a combination of appropriate media to deliver your message successfully.

4.3

Decide who needs to know what

The phrase 'need to know' originated in the armed forces to ensure that only people with a genuine need to know something are informed about it. It was a criterion used for classifying documents as 'Secret'.

One of the biggest challenges for a team manager is deciding who needs to know what. You have to give people enough information to allow them to make judgements and motivate themselves, but you mustn't give them so much information that they cannot absorb it all or slow down on work because they are so busy getting information.

As regards the first aspect of deciding who needs to know what you must consider this in relation to a person's capacity for action.
■ **If you know something you must act on that knowledge.** For example, imagine you have a team member who is responsible for selling your product or service. You become aware that a large potential client is going to move into the area. Once you inform the salesperson they have to act. They might act by approaching the prospect immediately, or they might delay an approach until the prospect actually arrives in the area, or they might choose *not* to do anything with the information (note that choosing is itself an action).

"Everybody gets so much information all day long that they lose their common sense"

Gertrude Stein, American writer

■ **If you don't know something you cannot act on that knowledge.** In the same example, if no one knows that the prospective client is moving in, no one can take any action at all. The caveat here is that if you know that a prospect is moving in but you act by choosing not to tell the sales person, then you may be suspected of having a 'hidden agenda'.

As regards the second aspect of giving too much information you must exercise judgement:

■ Avoid putting more than is absolutely necessary into the agenda of meetings.

■ Manage meeting agendas carefully to avoid overkill of data sharing.

■ Avoid bringing people into meetings where there is nothing of relevance to them.

■ Support your team in avoiding other meetings outside the team to which they are invited for no valuable purpose.

■ Keep the data display in the team area up to date.

■ Avoid cc and bcc emails and memos when unnecessary, and stop or question other people who use them habitually.

■ If appropriate, ask specified team members to select articles from relevant trade papers to be scrap-booked rather than distributing whole magazines to everyone.

Give an appropriate level of information for the person and situation.

Listen to your team

Who knows best about the minutiae of a team member's job? Who sees the problems that lie in the way of success on a day-to-day basis? Who spends time thinking of quicker, easier and better ways to do their job? Your team members are building up their experiences, and you should listen to them to make your own job easier.

There is a sad, vicious cycle that many managers get stuck in, which goes like this:

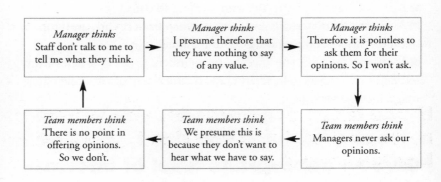

Manager thinks
Staff don't talk to me to tell me what they think.

Manager thinks
I presume therefore that they have nothing to say of any value.

Manager thinks
Therefore it is pointless to ask them for their opinions. So I won't ask.

Team members think
There is no point in offering opinions. So we don't.

Team members think
We presume this is because they don't want to hear what we have to say.

Team members think
Managers never ask our opinions.

To prevent this from happening, and to get out of this type of cycle if you are already in it, you need to do two things:

1 **Create an environment where team members are willing to speak.** You have to ask for opinions, feedback, suggestions, ideas, comments and thoughts. You have to make it easy for them to actually give you their input. This means you need to be accessible: give people your mobile number phone, your email address, have your door open, spend time at their workplace, eat with them, have coffee with them. Make it clear that any means of communication is acceptable.

2 **Prove that you genuinely listen.** You have to take the time (or make the time by booking an appointment) to dedicate to the team member talking to you. Answer your phone, respond to emails, don't scowl at people when they try to talk to you, avoid permanently surrounding yourself with senior peers who aren't members of your team. Listen and summarize team members' points, and question them intelligently about their opinions. Ask them to discuss things further or investigate. Always thank them for their time and contribution. Act appropriately on their input. Give credit where it is due. If their suggestion or idea isn't going to be implemented, then explain why.

Be persistent: if you are already in the cycle opposite it will take time to convince people that you want to change it.

If you listen to your team you will be more successful; if you don't, you'll be less successful.

4.5

Don't forget the remote people

Some team members may be in different parts of your building, some may be in different offices, some may be in different countries. In certain circumstances some may even be working in client offices or 'competitor' sites if you have a joint venture. These people need to be managed carefully.

It is increasingly the case that organizations work in matrices – they have cross-functional teams, staff on temporary secondments, 'in-country' staff nearer to markets than head office – or they engage in joint ventures or contract out their staff to clients. In all of these situations you have team members who may not see you or another member of the team for months on end. When a team member, or group of team members, is physically isolated like this it is very easy for them to feel that they are no longer part of the team. This can lead to divided loyalty, lack of support, resentment and stress.

Managing people who are remote is no different to managing a physically close team, except that you have to remember to do it (out of sight being out of mind!) and it is just harder. Here are some recommendations for managing people who are remote:

1 **Create and follow specific communication plans.** Have a plan so people know how often they should expect to contact or hear from you, in what medium and with what type of information. Also have a decision-making plan that clearly sets out the process for levels of autonomy and authority. Have a strategy for conflict resolution and/or escalation so your remote people know what to do if something isn't going right.

2 **Get to know your team members.** Arranging occasional face-to-face meetings or video conferencing calls is essential. If you wouldn't even recognize your remote team member then the likelihood is they don't feel much loyalty back to you or the team. Relying more on phone calls and emails is ok when you know each other better.

3 **Stay in touch.** Regularly get feedback about progress and life in general. Get the remote people involved in the GRIPS assessments (Secret 2.8). Contact people "just to say hi and how's it going?" Ask what support people want. Keep these people informed about what is going on elsewhere in the team.

4 **Maximize meetings.** When you hold a meeting make it as valuable as you can. Set an agenda and stick to it, but socialize as well.

5 **Use all the technology available to you.** Shaking someone's hand is better than just seeing their face. Seeing someone's face is better than just hearing a voice. Hearing a voice is better than just reading words. Reading words is better than just knowing that a team member or leader exists.

Support your team wherever they are.

4.6

Give your team some publicity

To keep your team functioning you need your boss's support. Your boss can allocate resources to your team, control the supply of tasks, and protect your team when times are tough. You therefore need to constantly remind your boss of the great job your team is doing.

Your boss may be co-located or remote from you and your team's location. Whichever is the case, don't take it for granted that your boss can see how much effort and success is being made.

Take every opportunity to update your boss on team progress and activity. These updates can be in written form via a formal report, email, memo or even text message, or you can set up a regular reporting meeting, even if it is just a brief 'touch base' over a coffee for ten minutes one day each week.

■ **Give specific data about activities and output.** Hours worked, milestones reached and successes achieved.
■ **Include developmental activities.** Training attended, qualifications achieved.

"A little self-promotion never hurt anybody" Wile E Coyote, cartoon character

■ **Pass on any positive customer feedback.** The boss can see the external value added by your team.

■ **Mention team members by name.** Give specific commendation either for effort or results.

■ **Highlight any suggestions made by team members.** Mention any plans the team has for improving business processes, services or conditions, especially if these are likely to be low-cost or no-cost plans.

■ **Invite feedback from the boss.** Pass on as much as is appropriate to the team or to individuals.

■ **Invite the boss to speak occasionally at team meetings.** This could be either simply to come along and show appreciation or to talk about organizational plans.

■ **Your success reflects upon your boss too.** He or she is likely to pass on some of this information elsewhere in your organization and possibly externally, thus increasing the power of the PR.

■ **Generate PR outside the immediate line of management.** Offer to speak to other parts of the organization about what your team does, or get team member to do this as a developmental activity.

■ **Offer clients and community groups the opportunity to come and see what you do.** You may not think that your job is very exciting but local schools will probably appreciate the career interest aspect. Charity organizations love to network with other organizations.

■ **Submit articles to local and trade press.** These again are valuable PR for your team that will make the team members feel appreciated, will raise your stock locally and within the organization and act as free recruitment advertising for your team.

Take every opportunity to generate positive PR for your team.

Protect and serve your team

A real team manager works for the team. Without a team there is no job for a manager, so the manager's role is to be a 'servant leader' to the team. In this chapter you will learn about creating trust, how to support your team and individuals, to lead by example and manage effectively when you have to deal with tricky situations.

5.1

Know who is working for whom

This may seem an odd comment, but without the team you have no job. 'Servant leadership' is the recognition that the job of the leader is to serve the group rather than that the job of the group is to serve the leader.

Servant leaders consider themselves 'first among equals'. This belief is at the very heart of servant leadership. The servant leader does not consider him or herself above the team they manage, but beside them. The servant leader values fellow team members as peers – people who help and learn from each other.

Are you a servant leader?
Consider each of the following questions: if you can genuinely answer with a "yes" to more than eight of these, you may be well on your way to becoming a servant leader.

■ Are you willing to sacrifice your own self-interest for the good of the team?
■ Do people in your team believe that you want to hear others' ideas and that you will value them?

"The highest type of ruler is one of whose existence the people are barely aware. Next comes one whom they love and praise. Next comes one whom they fear. Next comes one whom they despise and defy. When you are lacking in faith, others will be unfaithful to you."

Attributed to Lao-Tzu, Ancient Chinese philosopher

■ Do other team members believe that you understand what is happening in their lives and how it affects them?

■ Do they come to you in the belief that you care when something gets tough for them, at work or at home?

■ Do members of your team believe that you have a strong awareness for what is going on around you?

■ Do others follow your requests because they want to as opposed to because they have to?

■ Do others communicate their ideas when you are around, rather than going quiet when you are around?

■ Do others have confidence in your ability to anticipate the future and its consequences?

■ Do others believe you are preparing and helping the team to make a more positive contribution?

■ Do all people in the team believe that you are committed to helping them to develop and grow?

The questions above are worded for self-assessment. Obviously to know what the team actually thinks, as opposed to what you think the team thinks, you should ask them!

Being a servant leader makes people want to follow you rather than having to be dragged behind.

5.2

Build and keep trust

If you can't trust your team then you will not be confident that they will work without you watching. If they can't trust you, then they won't believe that you are worth working for. Trust, however, has to be earned initially and then earned regularly. Lose trust once and it takes a long time to earn it back.

As the team manager, there are some actions you can deliberately take to generate trust rather than simply waiting for it to evolve.

■ Trust levels rise when people feel that they are well informed. Share knowledge openly and freely (Secret 4.3). Do this verbally and in person rather than just sending emails and providing documents – people often haven't the time or inclination to read reams of paper.

> **case study** On a Wednesday a team manager said to the team that if they worked over the weekend to get a special project completed, then he would give them all two days' free holiday the following week to make up for it. On Friday morning one of the team put in a leave application to take his two free days on Thursday and Friday of the following week, having booked a

"Trust is the highest form of human motivation... But it takes time and patience"

Steven Covey, motivational author

Share also your opinions and humanity (if your team know nothing of your private life then you will always be relatively remote to them).

■ **Trust levels rise when people feel that they can express themselves openly.** Encourage team members to share their opinions and private thoughts regarding the team's purpose, processes, performance and future. Encourage this formally, through team briefings (Secret 4.1) and GRIPS (Secret 2.8) as well as informally.

■ **Trust levels rise when performance reliability is proven.** Initially manage expectations (for example, "I'll try to speak to the Managing Director before the end of the week" is more possible for you to fulfil than "I'll speak to the MD and get that authorized by the end of the week", which is outside your power. Having managed the expectations, keep your promises! And do this every time – things that seem unimportant to you may be critical to team members.

You earn trust through your behaviours, not your rank or position.

bargain long weekend holiday for his family. The team manager signed the leave application after the weekend, but senior managers returned it as "Request Denied" because the organization's policy required people to give a week's notice of holiday requests. The team member lost his deposit on the flights and accommodation, let alone his trust in the manager.

5.3

Lead by example

"Don't do as I do, do as I say" is seldom a good way to manage; it smacks of hypocrisy. If you want your team to behave in a certain way then you have to behave in that way yourself. You have to work to the same standards you want from them.

Leading by example DOESN'T mean that...

■ ...you have to be better at each role in your team than everyone else.
■ ...you need actually to have been employed in every or any of the jobs that your team members do.
■ ...you have to work longer hours than anyone else.
■ ...you should praise people even when they do badly.
■ ...you must earn the same money as the lowest paid of your team.
■ ...you have to run your team as a democracy, always seeking and going with the majority opinion.
■ ...you cannot change your mind if there's a sound reason for doing so.

Set an example and then, when people imitate you, you can be flattered.

Leading by example DOES mean that...

If you want people to...	You have to...
...use their initiative to solve problems.	....tell them that they can use their initiative, encourage them to do so, give them the resources to do so and reward them when they have done so.
...behave in an honest way.	...be seen to be honest with them, not just telling the truth but also ensuring that you do not keep back anything that is potentially harmful to your situation (being 'economical with the truth') and accept their honesty with good grace, even when it hurts you personally or creates difficulties.
...treat everything with integrity.	...have the highest standards of personal integrity yourself and treat any lack of integrity in others as an offence. Don't just abide by the 'word of the law', also abide by the spirit of the law as well.
...help each other (and you) out.	...help people out yourself when help is needed.
...fulfil their objectives.	...articulate those objectives clearly and precisely and then support the team in fulfilling them. Also articulate to the team what your objectives are and then be seen to be fulfilling them.
...stretch themselves to reach their full potential, attend training and learn from their experience.	...stretch yourself, undertake suitable training. You can always learn new things or get better at things you do.
...do as they are told.	...be seen to be doing so yourself.
...be positive and optimistic.	...exude optimism yourself in everything you say and do. Be smiley, look for the positive side, have self-belief.
...accept and respond to your feedback effectively.	...firstly accept their feedback about you and your management style, secondly thank them for it, thirdly react to that feedback in a developmental way and finally be seen to have changed as a result of it.

5.4

Support your team as a whole

As a team manager, you need treat your team as a whole, thinking of them as a unit that needs to be protected. That is your job and if you don't do it, no one will. (Treating your team as individuals is covered in Secret 5.5.)

Although you have your boss to keep happy and probably customers as well, you have to be entirely fair in order to protect your team. If a customer makes a complaint you must investigate it impartially. If your team is in the right you must support and stand by the team, regardless of the adage that the 'customer is always right'. Likewise, if a proposal is made by senior managers to break up your team, or merge it, move it or change anything about it, then it is your job to protect the team from harm. This doesn't mean fighting change:

case study A manager of a team of 20 actively encouraged social activities. After a few months, though, she realized that a subgroup of eight young men from the team had formed, through activities such as 5-a-side football, pub drinking sessions, paintball

it means assessing and analysing the proposal and making as much effort as you possibly can to ensure that the team comes out better equipped to fulfil its objectives. This may well mean that some individuals in the team have to suffer for the benefit of the team as a whole; if this is the case see Secret 5.5.

If the workload (which tends to be allocated down from above in most organizational hierarchies) is becoming too great or deadlines are being set too tight, it is your job to ensure that you manage upwards to keep the team functioning effectively. Simply accepting unreasonable demands and managing your team to achieve massive workloads or extreme deadlines is pointless if the team is too exhausted to carry on.

Even when everything is going smoothly you have to support the team actively.

■ **Organize or encourage team activity and team meetings.**
Ensure that the team members don't get into a blinkered 'just doing my job' approach. Watch out for breakaway subgroups within the team. Make sure that remote staff are included.

■ **Encourage social interaction.** Whether this is out of working hours or not, it is a good way for people to get to know each other better, which encourages more communication and interdependence. But beware the development of overly strong subgroups in this instance.

The whole team needs your active support at all times.

weekends and go-carting. The bonding within the subgroup was beginning to exclude other team members to the detriment of the whole team. The manager encouraged the organization of some alternative activities that were more attractive to the whole team.

5.5

Support your individuals

In addition to supporting your team as a unit you also have to recognize that you are dealing with individuals, each of whom has unique needs as well as unique skills to bring to the team. Treat them with respect while you consider what's best for the team. Bear in mind these points.

■ If a team member has a personal problem you might need to help them sort it out so that they can continue working.
■ If a customer complains about an individual you must investigate it impartially and stand by your team member if they are in the right.

case study A team manager inherited a team from a predecessor. One particular team member shone out as a high achiever. During an early one-to-one meeting the manager discovered that this team member had been asking for a transfer to a highly regarded specialist team for over two years, but that the previous manager wouldn't support the recommendation for

■ If a dispute arises between two team members you must be the arbitrator who reaches a fair decision and then enforces it equitably. (Your team ground rules will help here; see Secret 2.5.)

■ If someone has to lose their job through no fault of their own, then give them as much notice as you can and support them to find a new job. (This will minimize 'survivor syndrome'; see Secret 6.2.)

■ Acknowledge high performance from individuals; don't give a team bonus for one person's effort. If you do, it will reduce motivation.

■ If a team member is not performing well, don't give a collective punishment or impose collective monitoring; it will make the whole team hate you and the poor performer. Deal with poor performance with one-to-one coaching or individual supervision.

■ Not everyone will be motivated by the same things. Get to know your team members and what they each want out of life. This will allow you to recognize the things that will or will not motivate each person. You can then balance the needs of the team with the wants of the individuals.

■ Be prepared to support an individual even if it makes your role harder as the team manager.

Keep reminding yourself that everyone in your team is a unique individual.

fear of having to find a high-calibre replacement. The new manager immediately recommended the transfer the team member wanted. The team member was assessed and selected for the transfer and the whole team basked in the reflected glory. High-calibre potential recruits bombarded the manager with requests to join his winning team.

5.6

Manage the creative tension

Creative tension is a situation where disagreement or discord ultimately gives rise to better ideas or outcomes. Discord can simply be the difference between what we do now and what we could do, or it could be actual tension and disagreement between two or more people.

As the team manager it is your job to get the best out of the team and sometimes that is achieved by allowing, encouraging or setting up some creative tension. Here are two ways to manage creative tension.

1 **Create two opposing viewpoints.** Divide the team into two groups and get the groups to debate the motion: "We believe that this team operates in the most effective way it possibly could." One group is supporting the motion, arguing that every-

case study A manager tasked several pairs of team members to investigate a possible improvement to the physical security of the team in a hostile environment. Each pair had to present their solutions to the others

thing is as effective as possible, and the other group is arguing against the motion, specifically looking for aspects of the team's functions that could be improved. In order to produce cohesive arguments both teams have to analyse the methods and outputs of the team as a whole and compare them against alternatives. By the end of the debate you will have started people looking at and identifying ways to get better as a team.

2 **Create a group tasked with problem-solving and a third party to act as coach to them.** Whenever there is any internal complaint about an internal process, task the complainer and the people who do the process to work together to overcome the problem. The two sides now have a common goal: to improve the process to mutual benefit. Task a third party to act as a coach to them and set an improvement target, such as to produce more, or to reduce cost, time, resource use, as is appropriate. All parties then work together to devise a mutually acceptable solution, which, subject to your agreement, can then be put into place. (Your approval is only needed to act as a check that by improving this element of the team's work nothing else is jeopardized.) Since both sides have their own vested interest in a solution that works and it is developed jointly, you have a much better chance that it will be a successful solution.

You don't have to go out of your way to create tension but you can manage creative tension to everyone's benefit.

and face questions and challenges. At the end, the team manager selected what she deemed the best solutions and instigated them, rewarding the originators to mass applause from the rest of the team.

5.7

Don't encourage 'prima donnas'

Originally used in opera companies, the term 'prima donna' is Italian for 'first lady', designating the leading female singer to whom prime roles would be automatically given. These prima donnas were often regarded as egotistical, unreasonable and irritable.

If you allow any team members to turn into 'prima donnas', not only will they become unpopular but so will you. You will be perceived as being unduly influenced by the prima donna and therefore incon-

case study The manager of an estate agency took his staff for some teambuilding at a hotel in a picturesque tourist spot. The plan was to arrive the evening before for dinner and a bonding session in the bar. The manager's top-billing agent didn't show up for dinner, though, nor even for breakfast! As the manager opened the first morning session, he started receiving critical comments from the other agents about the missing agent. It became clear to the manager that the majority of the team felt that it was as much the manager's fault that the missing

sistent in your management. Some managers justify having a prima donna in order to maximize on the individual motivation of a high achiever. However, when other team members are feeling uncomfortable then you are out of balance – the team will probably fragment, with you and the prima donna outside it.

■ Ensure that you manage prima donna behaviour in the same way you would manage any unacceptable behaviour within your team.
■ Your team ground rules (Secret 2.5) should actually prohibit the symptoms of someone becoming a prima donna. Point this out to anyone who starts behaving as if they are better than the others.
■ Many managers are reluctant to discipline their highest achievers for fear of losing them to the competition. This is understandable, but acceptance of prima donna behaviour simply reinforces the belief that the prima donna can behave in this way.
■ Any prima donna behaviour must be dealt with quickly, discreetly and firmly, with the consequences of continuing spelt out clearly.

There is no place in a team for people who think they are inherently better than their team mates.

agent behaved like a prima donna – he always allowed him to bend the rules. Then the fellow finally arrived, all smiles and no apologies for being late. Deathly silence ensued until the manager made it clear to the errant agent that his lateness was not acceptable. The agent's response was to bluster and threaten to go to the opposition. At lunchtime, the manager took him aside and explained how his behaviour was destroying the team. After some reflection, the agent toned down his behaviour, and confidence rose in the team as a whole after this.

5.8

Manage your own boss

If your boss is a weak manager of you, then it is very much harder for you to manage your own team well. Consequently, the best team managers are those who are good at managing 'upwards' as well as 'downwards'.

Managing your boss is not, however, the easiest thing in the world, especially if your boss hasn't read this book! In order to manage your boss successfully you must be assertive; this means that you must stand up for your (and your team's) rights, while at the same time taking on all the appropriate responsibilities.

How to manage your boss pro-actively

■ Check that the 'bigger picture' issues of organizational or departmental vision and mission exist or are still relevant.

■ Ask your boss for measures of appreciation: "Are we doing the right things?" "Have we succeeded?" "Is this output acceptable?"

■ Tell your boss about your team's successes: targets achieved, accolades received, personal goals surpassed, personal news.

■ Keep your boss updated about progress.

one minute wonder Don't be afraid to reiterate a point or explain the consequences of something in more detail to your boss. These two simple strategies are very effective when it comes to asserting yourself.

■ Inform your boss early about potential problems, shortfalls or failures. This early warning allows the boss to react by providing support; without knowledge he or she cannot act.

How to manage your boss re-actively

■ Seek out clarification of all aspects of the objectives being passed down. Exactly what output is desired and acceptable, when is it needed by, how will success be measured, who else is affected by this objective?

■ Challenge any objectives that are genuinely excessively difficult to achieve, either in magnitude or timescale.

■ Probe any requests or demands that are inadequate in detail. "What exactly do you mean by 'sort it out'?" "When you say you want an acceptable return on investment, what would you consider acceptable?" "When you say by the end of the year, is that calendar year or financial year?"

■ When you inform your boss about potential problems, ask for his or her support.

■ Repeat yourself if the response from the manager seems to brush off the issue.

■ Explain the consequences of an action taken (or inaction). These can be negative, such as "the customer will complain" or "we will get sued". Or they can be positive, such as "we will succeed", "the customer will still buy from us" or "we will stay out of court".

If you don't manage your boss, no one else will, and your team will suffer.

5.9

'Manage out' uncooperative people

Sometimes you get someone who won't work well with the team no matter what motivational tactics you adopt. This person damages the morale and productivity of the whole team, and ultimately therefore has to be removed from the team.

Sometimes you recruit someone and it rapidly becomes clear that this person doesn't fit in. Sometimes a long-serving team member develops a loner attitude. It could be a personality issue with another team member, a grudge held over a specific incident or a general lack of respect for another team member. It could simply be a lack of understanding about the value of the team ethos. Whatever the cause, it cannot be allowed to continue indefinitely.

Your first approach should be to try to get things back on track. Discuss the matter privately with the person and get to the root cause of the issue. Look for solutions that will benefit the team as a whole by helping to bind them together happily. If the problem is one of personality or behaviour and attitude from other team members towards this individual then you need to deal with this (Secrets 5.5 and 5.6). But if the person simply won't work with the other team members then they are, by default, damaging the team, and they need to go.

If you are unable to remove the uncooperative person easily (e.g. by transferring them elsewhere or not renewing their contract), then 'managing out' can be an appropriate and sensitive way of persuading an employee to leave of their own accord. You need to sit down privately with the person and question them in such a way that they see for themselves that they need to take positive action in their life rather than just passing time unhappily on your team.

Here are some **closed questions** you can put to such a person.
■ Is it worth your while being unhappy having to work alongside people you don't want to work with?
■ Do you want to work with people who you don't trust?
■ Do you feel that the other team members respect and like you?
■ Is your career advancing while you are here but not part of the team?
■ Do you think that I can honestly report that you are performing well as a team member?
■ Are you achieving the best you could in life?

If the answer is "no" to any of these questions then the individual will probably see the value in moving on voluntarily.

Here are some **open questions** to put to this person to start them thinking about a positive future.
■ What type of job/employer/team mates would make you happy?
■ What things would you put on a CV to present to another employer?
■ What could I genuinely put in an employment reference for you?
■ When would be the best time for you to move to another job?

The next chapter includes situations when you have to say goodbye to people you would ideally prefer to keep on your team!

Ultimately you have to 'manage out' people who won't work within the team; otherwise you don't have a team.

Manage team changes

One thing is certain in the modern world – nothing stays the same for long. In this chapter you will learn how to manage change, in particular change that involves cutting down the size of your team and making redundancies. It covers the symptoms and problems of 'survivor syndrome', the importance of taking positive action from the moment change is earmarked, and how to rebuild your team after losing people.

6.1

Learn to let go

There are times as a team manager when you have to let people go, even if you would prefer to keep them. It can also be called lay-offs, downsizing, rightsizing, redundancies, streamlining, RIFting (Reduction In Force) or any other euphemism. Here are tips about doing the deed with as much sensitivity as possible.

Firstly make sure that your people know the situation, such as if you have been instructed to cut your team size by 10%. If you hide it and the team finds out, then you will have broken the bond of trust. Don't raise false hopes either by saying it might not happen. Here are some ways to reach the difficult decision about who goes.

■ **LIFO = Last In, First Out.** People who joined most recently are often chosen as the first in the line to leave.

■ **Call for volunteers.** This is especially appropriate if you can offer advantageous terms such as an enhanced pension or redundancy payment.

■ **Assessment.** Some organizations undertake an assessment of the current staff with a view to identifying who best to let go. You might have to carry out this assessment yourself. It is very hard to be totally objective, which means that whoever you choose might justifiably feel that it is unfair. (The only impartial way is to draw lots!)

Depending on the employment law in your country you will have different rules to comply with regarding unfair discrimination, and you must ensure that you stay on the right side of the law.

Breaking the bad news to people is a thankless task, so the only way to approach it is to try to make it as humane as possible.

■ Prepare for the redundancy meeting by reviewing personal information on the team member concerned. For example, is the day chosen to break the news the person's birthday? Has the person recently suffered any other trauma? Awareness of such matters can help you tread more sensitively and so minimize potential damage.

■ Ensure that a quiet, private location is available.

■ Conduct the meeting on a one-to-one basis, uninterrupted by telephone calls or messages of any sort. (If you need support from HR then run the meeting on just a two-to-one basis.)

■ Make every effort to inform the individual before anyone else knows.

■ Avoid breaking the news just before a holiday. People will have questions once the news has sunk in. Timing the interview during the day to suit individuals can also mean a lot to them.

■ In breaking the news that their employment is terminating, be brief and to the point. The meeting shouldn't take more than ten minutes: in this duration be clear about the date termination will take effect; about terms and conditions; working a notice period; and payments, benefits and security, if appropriate. Also make it clear what support you or the organization will offer the person: references, outplacement (see Jargon buster) or contracting work, as appropriate.

■ Say "thank you" and close the meeting.

Try to minimize the emotional effects of redundancy by being objective, honest and considerate.

6.2

Recognize survivor syndrome

'Survivor syndrome' is a potential effect on the team members who have not been laid off. There is no minimum number of people being made redundant that is required before the syndrome is triggered but the medium- and long-term effects are never good.

Symptoms of survivor syndrome may begin to appear within a matter of hours of the redundancy announcements. If the people who are losing their jobs are expected to work out notice periods, then this is a prime incubation period, as the survivors have a constant reminder of the impending disappearance of these colleagues.

If you observe any evidence of any of the symptoms listed here, suspect survivor syndrome. And don't forget that you are a survivor too, so these symptoms can be very close to home!

Symptoms and behaviours of survivor syndrome

■ Physical symptoms of stress, such as headaches, muscular tension, digestive problems.
■ Low morale, loss of sense of humour.
■ Irritability and mood swings.
■ Uncharacteristic lack of confidence in own abilities.

- Low self-esteem.
- Feelings of not being able to cope.
- Depressed, miserable or lethargic.
- Expressing feelings of insecurity about job.
- Fear of the unknown, shown by constant demands for assurance.
- Narrow-minded and risk averse.
- Increased resistance to change.
- Mistrust of management (look out for sudden silences when you appear).
- Low productivity.
- Increased absenteeism or lateness.
- Presentism (being physically present but not actually doing the job).
- Lack of loyalty to team, team mates, you or the organization.
- Loss of respect for organizational possessions (e.g. increases in graffiti, damage to company property).
- Acts of sabotage.

Studies by Cascio in 1993, Macky in 2004 and Gandolfi in 2008 all showed that where teams have downsized the longer term effects on results are negative. Studies by Vahtera and others in 2004 and by Røed and Fevang in 2007 found that teams that downsized saw an increase in the sickness absence rate and a decrease in the return to work rate.

Survivor syndrome leads to an easily measurable increase in absenteeism. It also leads to a number of other less easily measurable but equally undesirable effects: introversion and self-absorption, aversion to anything new, slow working, an absence of smiles and a loss of pride in the team. These are just as bad for the team manager because they make everyday work harder than it needs to be. The Secrets that follow show you how to manage survivor syndrome.

Survivor syndrome is real, and its effects on teams are bad. Learn to recognize the symptoms.

6.3

React sensibly to change

An article in the Journal of Managerial Psychology entitled 'Survivor Syndrome – A Management Myth?' set out a significant case study which showed that survivor syndrome is not inevitable. Sensible management can prevent the development of survivor syndrome and avoid its unfortunate effects.

As soon as you have an inkling of major change coming to your team, instigate this five-point strategy to avoid survivor syndrome.

1 **Communicate.** Tell people why the changes are necessary and how you think roles will change. Take time to explain that it is important now to plan to recover and grow and what role team members can play. Get the team involved in helping to plan.

2 **Plan.** Figure out how the redundancies will affect survivors and therefore what support and assistance will be needed from you and the organization. Schedule the reassignment of tasks and responsibilities. Training, resourcing, equipping and supporting will be vital to the re-growth of the team.

one minute wonder Remember to keep exuding optimism and celebrate all successes, even when others are glum. Recognize that you are a new team, so invest in teambuilding. Foster camaraderie and encourage group discussions and input. Don't over-promise; be honest. You will lose all trust if you say the redundancies are over, but then more occur.

3 Listen empathetically. Most survivors go through a traditional trauma cycle with periods of denial, anger, grieving and guilt before they reach a calmer acceptance and, therefore, an ability to move on and start to perform well. A manager who is able to console his or her team can help the team and individuals to reach this stage faster and, therefore, with less damage along the way. When your team members air their feelings, individually or in a group, be quiet and listen. Avoid response and judgement until you have heard and thought.

4 Rebuild trust. Redundancies break the 'psychological contract' of trust. Rebuild trust by demonstrating care, listening to concerns, acting with humanity and integrity, leading by example and always offering support.

5 Commit to developing survivors' skills. With reassigned responsibilities and rising workloads, team members may need additional training, coaching and advice. Expect this, plan for it and commit to it. Reading books, peer coaching, manager coaching, e-learning and on-the-job training from colleagues are all ways to develop skills and abilities without high expenditure.

Use this five-point plan to stop survivor syndrome from developing.

6.4

Take the first step to manage survivors

The first step to managing survivors is to get them to air their opinions and feelings and get their emotions off their chests. The whole team, you included, might benefit from a 'pity party'.

A 'pity party' – whether held in a room at the office or at an external venue – gives you the opportunity to exhibit empathy and to encourage and receive some feedback. It show that you value your team members as people. For team members it gives the opportunity to get things out in the open rather than bottling them up or having conversations behind your back.

Start by having a discussion about their (and your) general emotions, then move to the specific likely sources of future pain – changed work patterns, higher workloads, fewer colleagues, certain people they might miss or whatever.

■ Ask open questions; try not to ask leading questions that might stifle genuine offerings.
■ Pay attention to peoples' responses.

■ Make it clear that you are taking great pains to listen and that you care about how people feel.

■ Pay attention to people who are reluctant to respond.

Be warned, though: at some point, you may well come under attack. Don't be defensive. Remember the intention was to establish your empathy. Instead, accept the attacks with an apology and explain that you appreciate that the changes may have been horrible for people. Don't try to elicit sympathy for yourself in any way – for example by mentioning your suffering in being the bearer of bad news or the person who had to make the tough decision; it won't look good. No one loves the executioner who claims he was just following orders or doing his job.

■ Move the discussion on to get suggestions as to how you can make it easier for the team to perform under the new circumstances.

■ Get a brainstorm going to generate a list of actions you can take to help your team.

■ Ask the team to prioritize the list.

■ Wrap up by committing to do everything you can to action the suggestions the team has generated, and thank them for their contributions.

Every item on the team's list that you address will have a major effect in helping them to recognize the value they have and the fact that the team is moving forward. It will also raise your stock as a member of the team and its manager.

First bring the emotions about redundancy under control so you can then deal with the practicalities.

6.5

Follow up the survivor management

Once you have taken the first step outlined in Secret 6.4, you have to keep it all going. Now is the time to invest heavily in managing the new team, not just the targets and results but also the teamwork and the team as individuals. Fail to do this and it will all fall apart into survivor syndrome.

The traditional reaction to major change, especially redundancies, is to cut back on everything. Sadly this creates and reinforces an appearance of a total lack of confidence in the future and an inability to manage more than one thing at once.

■ There are two areas where you should be investing: people and the environment in which they operate.

■ Investment may require spending money or it may be simply putting effort, time and thought into things.

Ways to invest in the people in your surviving team	Ways to invest in the environment in which your surviving team works
Continue to run social events and functions, e.g. birthdays.	Redecorate.
Invest in training and development. Continue to develop people for promotion even though the actual promotion may not be possible.	Replace worn out furniture.
Take time to coach people.	Upgrade equipment.
Set up a buddying system or mentoring scheme for people taking on new responsibilities.	Engage in active Public Relations, such as information sessions for the organization and customers. Run careers days.
Promote people who are worthy of it. If you can only give them acting promotions at present, then backdate the seniority and the pay when you can.	Start or keep advertising; maintain any sponsorship that you are involved in.
Celebrate every success and achievement, not just the results and targets but also the things off the list you generated in Secret 6.4.	Don't slash any socially responsible activity you may have been undertaking. The feel-good factor and the PR value create confidence.

If you have to, find ways of doing these things for less money, but don't stop investing; if you do you will probably be cutting off your nose to spite your face. If the authority to spend money isn't within your power then you must try to influence your boss to agree that the spending is worthwhile.

Don't cut back now or you increase the appearance of being unable to cope.

Disband your team

Regardless of the reasons for the team's cessation – project completion, staff rotation or obsolescence of tasks – it is worth doing it thoughtfully. Sensible planning for the wind down ensures that everyone benefits: you personally, each team member and the organization as a whole. This chapter will help you to disband your team positively.

7.1

Prepare to say goodbye

It is said that good advance planning prevents poor performance and this is just as true in disbanding as elsewhere in the management of teams. It is important that everyone in the team has time to prepare for the ending of the team, both on a psychological and a practical basis.

Team members must have as much notice as possible of the intended disbandment (see Secret 4.3). This allows people to get used to the idea and, if necessary, to start to plan for their individual future.

Many managers feel that by letting people start to plan for their future they are distracted from the present, which can lower productivity. There is logic in this argument; the solution is to ensure that the team will have a short breathing space after completion of the task.

■ **Handing over.** There will be many cases where a team needs to hand over its product to other people, which has to be planned and executed logically and completely. For example, if the team is developing software, it needs to hand over all the documentation, testing results, codes and user manuals to the user or the future maintenance people.

■ **Equipment and material.** The team members might hold equipment, tools, data or cash that is the property of the organization. This will need to be returned if team members are leaving the organization as well as the team.

■ **Employment benefits.** Team members might also hold certain tangible and intangible employment benefits such as credit cards, expense accounts, a company car, health insurance policy or pension fund. It is critically important that the future of these items is clearly known and managed.

■ **The sendoff.** On a team basis you will want to organize a decent send off for the people you have worked alongside. In one of my previous employers, where teams were formed and disbanded on a yearly basis, team members contributed a small sum of money each week towards a 'wake fund'. This meant that by the time the disbandment came we had a significant fund for a goodbye party.

■ **The learning log.** It is always worth reflecting and learning from any experience in life, good, bad or mixed. Give people notice that you want to collate a 'learning log' from the team. This gives everyone time to reflect individually on what the experience has taught them, and to discuss informally with their colleagues. This will make your learning log far richer when you come to create it. (See Secret 7.3.)

Take the time to give notice and plan a proper goodbye.

7.2

Celebrate success

Just as a funeral is as much a celebration of a life as the expression of grief, the ending of a team's existence is usually tinged with conflicting emotions. You need to lead the event to ensure that it isn't just a sad occasion. Go out with a bang, not a whimper!

Whatever the reason your team is being disbanded, there must be something to celebrate. Even if you didn't win the world cup, you must have won something or have got better than you were at the start.

As the manager it is your role to make the ending of the team an opportunity for some celebration and recognition. You can select things yourself to reward or have the team nominate and vote for winners in various categories. Opposite are some ideas for gestures that have been used successfully in the past.

case study One team was short on funds so their awards were: A4 Certificates printed using Microsoft Word wizards; a Superman Tee-shirt for the elected 'super hero'; a box of Cadbury's Celebrations chocolates for each team member; a second-hand hand-bell mounted on a homemade plinth for the 'Team Member Who Dropped the Biggest Clanger'; and a toy

- A medal or award to be given to each team member as a token of recognition that they were part of a winning team.
- A team photo that is mounted and given to each team member.
- A practical item that has some sentimental value as well (for example a desk set or key fob with a commemorative plaque).
- A certificate of appreciation from a senior manager. This can be given to all or tailored specifically for certain people.
- Awards for specific actions or contributions. For example: Most Successful Sales Person, Person Who Clocked Most Hours on the Project, Most Helpful Team Member, Super-hero Award for...
- You can also have joke awards (but not sarcastic ones).

Arrange and hold a party that is suitable for the organization that you belong to. Do your best to get the whole team together, even if some people are not normally based at the same location. Ensure that the party is arranged (decoration, refreshments, location etc) as a joyous occasion rather than an afterthought. Make a speech, or get an organizational dignitary or appropriate customer to make a speech of appreciation. Have your awards ceremony at the party, and present them in such a way that allows for applause.

This could be the last time the team members see each other, so make it a good memory.

plastic bullet, painted silver and glued to a little wooden plate, for the 'Silver Bullet Award for Finding and Fixing the Biggest Problem'. They even awarded someone with the work knife he had used in his job on the team, mounted in a frame and awarded to 'The Sharpest Tool In the Box'. He never quite worked out if it was truly an accolade or not!

7.3

Learn from experience

Many organizations nowadays are embracing the idea of lifelong learning – the idea that we continue to learn throughout our lives, and as much from everyday activity as formal training. The disbanding of a team is a good time to reflect and learn.

You have to ask, even of yourself, open questions, not closed ones.

■ Ask "what did you learn?" rather than "did you learn anything?"
■ Ask "what does this teach us?" rather than "does this teach us anything?"

To help people along with this activity you should give team members something to focus on; one idea is to use the 'families' that are often used in cause and effect analysis. These are quite easy to remember because they all start with the letter M: **Material**, **Manpower**, **Method**, **Management** and **Machinery**.

We learn from both our successes and failures (together we call it 'experience'), by reflecting on specific things that happened.

Examples of learning from success

What did we do with the *manpower* that made it work?	We trained people before they were needed, meaning that they were productive from Day One.
What did we do with *machinery* that contributed to success?	Nothing that we don't usually do.
What was specific about our *method* that helped?	The detailed planning allowed us to have expertise and material ready on a Just-In-Time (JIT) basis.
How did our *management* help?	Our openness and willingness to face up to problems meant that we got them sorted out really quickly.
What about our *material*?	Using material B instead of material A allowed us to complete the task in half the time we expected.

Examples of learning from mistakes

What have we learned about our *method*?	The usual method would have prevented a certain problem, but we didn't follow the usual method.
What have we learned about *manpower*?	Team member X didn't follow the usual method, which gave rise to the problem.
What have we learned about *material*?	Team member X hasn't got a manual that explains the usual method, because he missed the induction training.
What have we learned about *management*?	We must make sure everyone is inducted properly.
What have we learned about *machinery*?	Nothing – all the tools are fine and kept in the right places.

Identify 'best practice' from the project.

7.4

Spread the word

By spreading the word that the team is being disbanded you are telling prospective employers and managers that there is talent looking for a home. This brings untold benefits to individual team members and possibly even the whole team. Spread the word both by networking and more formally.

1 Tell all team members that they can let all their business contacts know of the impending end of the team.

2 Formally notify the senior managers of all your clients and prospective clients that you will soon finish successfully.

case study A team in the finance industry was being disbanded; their employer had decided to pull out of the specific market that the team specialized in. The team manager informally spread the word among all the clients and suppliers that the team dealt with on a daily basis that it was being disbanded. He highlighted the successes the team had had over the years and

3 Formally notify all the senior managers in your own organization of your team's completion of tasks.

4 Invite a senior figure in the organization (and/or an important customer) to present awards.

5 Write up and disseminate your learning log internally and to clients and suppliers (make sure it is not commercially sensitive). Offer it to any relevant trade or professional bodies.

6 Use the learning log to form the basis of an article you can submit to in-house magazines, local press, trade journals, professional journals, websites or similar. If appropriate, offer it as case study material to students.

7 As and when your team members find new roles, publicize these anywhere you can, adding a mention that the team is being disbanded so there are other talented people available.

Inform other people in advance that you are finishing, so they can offer you and your colleagues new roles.

expressed their gratitude for support and custom. Within three weeks of his starting this networking PR campaign most of his team members had been approached by recruiters. In the fourth week he was contacted by an organization interested in taking on the whole team. They literally went from one employer to another with no break.

7.5

Keep in touch

It is often said that in order to get on in life it isn't a matter of what you know, but who you know. The world is absolutely full of alumni groups and friends reunited, let alone 'old boy networks' and Masonic lodges. People understandably like to do business with people they know and trust. Why not set up a little informal network from your team?

Keeping in touch used to be more difficult than it is nowadays. In the past if you lost your address book you lost touch, end of story. Now you probably synchronize your mobile phone with your desktop PC so it is almost impossible to lose your address book! Or if someone moved employer or home and forgot to tell you in the past, you would lose touch. Nowadays you can 'Google' someone and quite possibly find them in a matter of minutes.

case study I was a member of a team in 1985... my team leader came to work for me in 1988 in a different organization. I was on a big team in 1995... two of us kept in touch and formed our own team in 2007 because of that relationship. I worked on another team

> # "We are on a mission from God; we're putting the band back together" **Jake and Elwood Blues of The Blues Brothers**

Social networking websites abound that are global in reach. As people move not just within towns and counties but also internationally, they can still be found. These types of website cross borders allowing a person in Johannesburg to find ex-colleagues in the UK, Malaya, Jordan, Iraq and Australia (that is a genuine list). Twitter (twitter.com) can also be used to keep in touch with ex-team members.

It is always worthwhile to arrange an informal get-together of an old team. (This is where having a team photo with names on it really helps!) There may be direct benefits to individual team members, or even social family benefits. For example, a team had a 20-year reunion. One team member had a 19-year-old son who was just leaving college, having graduated in a very specific industry. Another team member was now employed in that industry and was happy to create some introductions to assist the youngster in networking for several companies.

People like to do business with people they know and trust, so keep in touch!

in 1997... the team manager added me to his team in 1999, 2001, 2005 and 2006... with three different employers. I worked for a customer in 1993... she became a teammate in 1994... in 1996 and 1998 I was part of the team she put together.

7.6

Provide 'after care' for your team

You may not have an official responsibility for your team after the disbandment, but it is always wise to provide some after care. The world is a small place, after all, and you may find yourself wanting to employ (or even be employed by) these people in the future.

■ As the team breaks up, ensure that you share any useful networking contacts with your people.

■ Be prepared to 'put in a good word' for your team members with appropriate potential benefactors.

■ Provide people with a written testimonial if they ask for one.

case study A team manager kept in touch with her team after they disbanded, providing references and advice to several members over the next couple of years. While taking a career break to start a family, she was involved in charity work for her children's school. One

■ Although your employer may have a fixed policy about testimonials and references, it doesn't mean that you cannot say whatever you want to as a private individual.

■ Be prepared to give team members your forwarding address details so that any future employer who wants a direct referee (rather than a pre-written testimonial, which can be easily forged and is therefore often rejected) can contact you.

■ Be the person who facilitates an informal get-together of the old team. You don't necessarily have to be the person who organizes it, just the person who suggests it to someone who can organize it, especially if you can provide a lot of the contact information.

■ Remember your old team mates when you have a need in the future, or when someone you know has a need. Don't be afraid to pass on their details or to call them yourself to make an introduction.

■ If you can, keep an eye on their careers and send them a letter of congratulations when they get a new job, win an award, announce a success or get married. You could even keep a note of birthdays and send a greeting each year.

You never know when you will want a favour, so keep people positive.

of her old members provided unwanted samples that the charity was able to use as prizes to raise funds. Another old member brought his entire new team to provide a free day's labour to the charity in return for some PR coverage in the local press.

Jargon buster

Ad hoc
A term meaning something created for this single purpose.

Brainstorm
A group activity where all ideas in response to a specified issue are recorded for consideration later. See www.businessballs.com/brainstorming.htm for more information.

CC/BCC = carbon copy
To provide or send a copy of a document to another person openly. BCC stands for blind carbon copy, which means to provide or send a copy of a document to another person without letting the main recipient know of the copy.

Cliques
Small informal groups, usually rather secretive or exclusive.

Closed question
A type of question where the answer can only be "yes", "no", or "I don't know". For example, "Is this a good idea?"

Complementary
Matching or corresponding to.

CV = curriculum vitae
The document that describes your work history, experience, skills and abilities in order to support an application for a job or work.

Data display
The act of publicly displaying data about the team's activities, for example a bulletin board displaying work in progress and allocation of staff to tasks.

Dotted line responsibilities
As opposed to (full) line responsibility, which is both functional and hierarchical, 'dotted line' is typical of a subsidiary relationship. For example, the Finance Manager has a full direct line responsibility to the General Manager and a dotted line responsibility to the Finance Director, who sets the procedures and functional details.

Employment reference
A testimonial provided by an employer or manager for an employee who is leaving in order to support their application for work in the future.

Interdependency
Reliance upon others.

Leading questions
A type of question where the desired answer is implicit in the question. For example, "You think this is a good idea, don't you?"

Matrix management

An organizational system where staff may have two managers – one functional and one operational. (See also dotted line responsibilities above.)

Networking

The act of making, exploiting and maintaining social contacts for business or personal benefit. Most professional associations run networking events for their members. Individual networking can include use of social networking sites on the Internet, though many employers view this as 'notworking' and ban it!

Open question

A type of question that demands the person think of a detailed answer. For example, "What do you think of this idea?"

Outplacement

A service provided (usually by the employer) to people being made redundant. It aims to help people to find new jobs or careers in the wake of their departure.

Peter Principle

The theory that in a hierarchical organiza-tion, an employee tends to be promoted in stages until reaching their personal level of incompetence.

Scrap booking

Running an in-house press cuttings service, which involves trawling publications for articles of interest and then creating a custom digest of relevant material.

Silo mentality

Also known as bunker mentality, this is the attitude that sees me and my immediate team as isolated from the rest of the organi-zation. It can be a result of snobbery or an inferiority complex, but whatever the cause it is almost always destructive.

Sinecure

An office or post or role or job that carries a salary but requires work of little or no real value.

SMART objectives

SMART is an acronym standing for Specific, Measurable, Achievable, Relevant and Timebound. It is a common base for many organizations' approach to goal or objective setting.

Utilization target

The target amount of time an individual is expected to bill to clients or projects. Often expressed as a percentage of the working period.

Further reading

On team leadership in general

Adair, John *Action Centred Leadership* (Gower, 1979) ISBN 978-0566021435

Adair, John *John Adair's 100 Greatest Ideas for Effective Leadership and Management* (Capstone, 2002) ISBN 978-1841121406

Belbin, R.M. *Management Teams: Why They Succeed or Fail* (Butterworth-Heinemann, 2010) ISBN 978-1856178075

Bennis, Warren G. and Nanus, Bert *Leadership: Strategies for Taking Charge* (Harper Business Essentials, 2003) ISBN 978-0060913366

Deschamps, Jean-Philippe *Innovation Leaders: How Senior Executives Stimulate, Steer and Sustain Innovation* (John Wiley and Sons, 2008) ISBN 978-0470515242

Fisher, Kimball and Mareen *The Distance Manager: A Hands on Guide to Managing Off-Site Employees and Virtual Teams* (McGraw-Hill Professional, 2000) ISBN 978-0071360654

Lencioni, Patrick *The Five Dysfunctions of a Team* (Jossey-Bass, 2002) ISBN 978-0787960759

McGregor, Douglas *Leadership and Motivation* (MIT Press, 1966) ISBN 978-0262130233

Michaelson, Gerald A. *Sun Tzu: The Art of War for Managers – 50 Strategic Rules* (Adams Media, 2001) ISBN 978-1580624596

Morrell, Shackleton and Capparell *Shackleton's Way: Leadership Lessons from the Great Antarctic Explorer* (Penguin, 2002) ISBN 978-0142002360

Nelson, Robert B. *Empowering Employees through Delegation* (Longman Higher Education, 1994) ISBN 978-0786301997

Pincus, Marilyn *Managing Difficult People: A Survival Guide for Handling Any Employee* (Adams Media, 2005) ISBN 978-1593371869

www.belbin.com

http://home.att.net/~coachthee/Archives/Colin_Powell_on_Leadership.html

www.spangehawe.co.uk/pdfs/The_Importance_of_Followership.pdf

On monkey management

http://workstar.net/library/monkey.htm

Blanchard, Oncken and Burrows *The One Minute Manager Meets The Monkey* (Morrow, 1989) ISBN 978-0688067670

On negativity and managing the miseries

pageshttp://humanresources.about.com/cs/conflictres/a/negativitycures.htm

Topchik, Gary *Managing Workplace Negativity* (Amacom, 2001) ISBN 978-0814405826

On setting expectations and praise

http://humanresources.about.com/od/managementtips/a/mgmtsecret.htm

On reward

Armstrong, Michael and Murlis, Helen *Reward Management: A Handbook of Remuneration Strategy and Practice* (Kogan Page, 2007) ISBN 978-0749449865

On team briefing

http://www.entrepreneur.com/tradejournals/article/100509058.html

On managing remote teams

http://blogs.techrepublic.com.com/itdojo/?p=124

This website has a bibliography of different books on servant leadership in different settings, for instance faith leaders, business, the military and education.

http://www.greenleaf.org/whatissl/SL-Bibliography.pdf

On trust

http://ezinearticles.com/?Trust:-A-Critical-Factor-to-Your-Teams-Success&id=57996

On survivor syndrome

Baruch, Yehuda and Hind, Patricia *Survivor Syndrome: A Management Myth?* (Journal of Managerial Psychology, 2000, Volume15, Issue 1, Pages 29–45) ISSN: 0268-3946

www.BusinessSecrets.net